Help
for the
Journey

Daily Devotions for Victorious Living

Ron and Ryan Sutton

Help for the Journey

ISBN: 978- 1546959557

ABOUT THE AUTHORS

Ron Sutton was converted from a life of crime and drug abuse during the Jesus Movement in 1972. His ministry has taken him to sixty nations. He has conducted mass crusades and leaders' conferences, served as a missionary, evangelist, pastor and church planter. His books on evangelism, gospel tracts and pro-life literature have been distributed throughout the USA and internationally. He and his wife Cindy established a drug rehabilitation ministry, a childrens' home in Costa Rica, and a home for unwed mothers. Ron served as director of the School of Christ International in Africa. He is currently planting a church near St. Louis, while continuing to travel in ministry, and assist his son Ryan at The Grace Center.

Ryan Sutton surrendered to the call to preach under the ministry of B.H. Clendennen a few days after his fourteenth birthday in 1997. He preached his first sermon the following Sunday and was ordained to pastor his first church three years later. He has preached in churches and revivals throughout the USA and has ministered internationally in China, Russia, India, Europe, Africa and Latin America. Ryan continues to travel and preach throughout the nation while serving as the senior pastor of The Grace Center, a dynamic multi-cultural church, in Festus, Missouri.

TO ORDER MATERIALS OR SCHEDULE MEETINGS

The Grace Center

P.O. Box 21, Crystal City, Missouri 63019

314-960-8308

www.TheGraceCenter.com | www.RyanSutton.org

Day One

"Thanks be unto God, which always causes us to triumph in Christ" (2 Corinthians 2:14 KJV).

Victory centers wholly in the Lord Jesus. You should be aware of your weakness and areas of need, but don't dwell too much on them. You should be aware of the power of your foe, but don't magnify it.

There are times when you must look away from your need. You must look away from your enemy. You must be absolutely taken up with the Lord Jesus – with His keeping power, with His conquering power, with the certainty of His victory and your share in it. You won't be discouraged when things go wrong, when the road gets rough, when there are delays or setbacks – if you remember – *"In all these things, we are more than conquerors through him that loved us"* (Romans 8:37 KJV).

"But thanks be to God, who gives us the victory through our Lord Jesus Christ. Therefore my beloved brethren be ye steadfast, unmovable, always abounding in the work of the Lord, for as much as you know that your labor is not in vain in the Lord" (1 Corinthians 15:57-58 KJV).

Day Two

Righteousness

Believers have been made righteous. God has declared us "Not guilty." That's why we can say with confidence, *"There is now no condemnation for those who are in Christ Jesus"* (Romans 8:1 NIV).

Righteousness means the ability to stand in the Father's presence without the sense of guilt or condemnation…Also, to be able to stand in the presence of Satan without the sense of inferiority or fear.

"But of him are ye in Christ Jesus, who of God is made unto us wisdom, and righteousness, and sanctification, and redemption" (1 Corinthians 1:30 KJV).

"For He made Him who knew no sin to be sin for us, that we might become the righteousness of God in Him" (2 Corinthians 5:21 NKJV).

You are righteous because of what Jesus did not because of what you do.

Day Three

Motivation

It's amazing what you can do when you are really motivated. I heard a story about the famous coach, Bear Bryant, who is known as a great motivator. During a crucial game his team was ahead by six points with only a minute left to play and they had the ball. It looked like the game was in the bag. Bryant sent in a running play to his quarterback, but the quarterback decided to disregard his coach's instructions and pass. He thought he would surprise the other team and catch them off guard. One of the defensive backs, who was one of the fastest runners in the league, intercepted the pass. The Alabama quarterback who had only average speed took off after the defensive back and caught him on the five yard line. Alabama won the game. After the game the opposing coach asked the quarterback, "How did you catch my man? You're not that fast." He responded, "Sir, how well do you know Coach Bryant? Your quarterback was running for a touchdown. I was running for my life!"

What makes you want to run the Christian race? What makes you want to be the best you can be for the glory of God? Someday you are going to stand before your "Coach". You won't need to fear because you're forgiven. But won't you want to hear Him say, "You ran well. You did your best. Well done good and faithful servant."

What Jesus did for you on the cross and what He is still doing for you today should motivate you to do your best, to be the best you can be. It's amazing what you can do when you're really motivated. I'm betting on you. I'll bet you can do better – if you want to.

"Do you not know that those who run in a race all run, but one receives the prize? Run in such a way that you may obtain it" (1 Corinthians 9:24 NKJV).

Day Four

Striving Valiantly

This quote from Theodore Roosevelt in 1899 has always challenged me to stay motivated:

"It is not critic who counts; not the man who points out how the strong man stumbled or where the doer of deeds could have them better. The credit belongs to the man who is actually in the arena; whose face is marred by dust and sweat and blood; who strives valiantly; who may err and come up short again and again, because there is no effort without error and shortcoming; the credit goes to the man who does actually try to do the deed; who knows the great enthusiasm, the great devotion and spends himself in a worthy cause; who at the worst, if he fails, at least fails while daring greatly. Far better it is to dare mighty things, to win glorious triumphs, even though checkered by failure, than to rank with those who neither enjoy much nor suffer much because they live in the gray twilight that knows neither victory nor defeat."

We're serving a great King. We're living for a great cause. We're doing a great work for God. There are no insignificant tasks in the King's business. God needs each of us. God has a purpose for you.

I challenge you to get in the arena, get involved, give God some time. Go for it! Do the best you can do. Be the best you can be.

"So I run with purpose in every step. I am not just shadowboxing" (1 Corinthians 9:26 NLT).

"Therefore I do not run like someone running aimlessly; I do not fight like a boxer beating the air. No, I strike a blow to my body and make it my slave so that after I have preached to others, I myself will not be disqualified for the prize" (1 Corinthians 9:26-27 NIV).

Day Five

Let Your Light Shine

Isaiah prophesied in Isaiah 60:2, *"Darkness as black as night shall cover all the people of the earth…"* (TLB).

I'm sure you would agree that some of that darkness is settling over the earth today. What should be the Christians' response?

Should we talk about how bad it is? How hopeless things are? Anybody can do that. If the lights go out in a room you don't need a prophet to say, "It's dark in here!" You need someone to flip a switch and turn the light on.

There is a positive side to Isaiah's prophecy, "…but the glory of the Lord will shine from you."

He challenges God's people to, *"Arise! Shine! For your light has come and the glory of the Lord has risen upon you"* (Isaiah 60:1 NKJV).

You can sit around and talk about how bad things are, how dark it is, if you want to. You won't help anybody and you will get depressed in the process. I'm going to turn on the light. I'm going to do what Jesus said we should do.

"Don't hide your light! Let it shine for all; let your good deeds glow for all to see, so that they will praise your Heavenly Father" (Matthew 5:15-16 LB).

Day Six

Faith and Patience

Do you know anyone who enjoys waiting? About the only thing I like to receive later than expected are bills.

But waiting is a fact of life. When we release our faith we like to see instant results, but there is usually a "waiting phase" between claiming God's promises and seeing them fulfilled.

We need to learn a lesson from the farmer. He doesn't get discouraged because there is a waiting phase between sowing and reaping. (James 4:7-8)

What we do during the waiting phase is the key to victory. Satan will try to discourage you, get you to doubt God's faithfulness, or steal your confidence.

I hope the following verse will help those of you who are waiting for God to come through for you.

"We do not want you to become lazy, but to imitate those who through faith and patience inherit what has been promised" (Hebrews 6:12 NIV).

Day Seven

Obstacle or Opportunity?

In ancient times, a king had a huge boulder placed in a roadway, then hid and watched to see if anyone would remove it. Some of the kingdom's biggest merchants and courtiers came by and simply walked around it. Many of them loudly blamed the king for not keeping the roads clear, but none of them did anything about getting the big stone out of the way.

Then a peasant farmer came along, carrying a load of vegetables on his back. When he came to the boulder, he laid down his burden and began trying to move it to the side of the road. After much straining and pushing he finally succeeded.

As he was picking up his vegetables he noticed a purse lying in the road where the boulder had been. The purse contained many gold pieces and a note from the king explaining that the gold was for the person who removed the stone from the road.

He learned what many others have learned since:

"Sometimes obstacles, present an opportunity to improve your condition."

"Then Caleb quieted the people before Moses, and said, 'Let us go up at once and take possession, for we are well able to overcome it'" (Numbers 13:30 NKJV).

Day Eight

Encourage Yourself in the Lord

The pressure is on right now. Everybody feels it – some more than others.

We need extra strength – supernatural strength – to overcome the spiritual heaviness and oppression that attack us.

The Bible tells us how to get it in 1 Samuel 30.

David had big problems. His enemies had destroyed his city, stolen his possessions and kidnapped his family while he was off fighting a war. He returned home to find nothing but smoldering ashes, and a heap of ruins. Everything he valued in life had been taken away.

"David was greatly distressed." (v. 6)

What do you do in moments like that?

"...but David encouraged himself in the Lord his God." (v. 6)

The encouragement you need in the hard times, the discouraging times, the stressful times can only come from a supernatural source. David found strength, hope, encouragement in God's presence.

"And David inquired of the Lord." (v. 8)

He spent time in prayer and the word.

David asked, *"Shall I pursue my enemies? Shall I overtake them?"*

God answered, *"Pursue! For you will surely overtake them and without fail recover all."*

Read the rest of 1 Samuel 30 and you will discover that David got back everything the enemy has stolen – plus interest!

Difficulty and distress from pressure and problems can be overcome with the strength we get from God's word.

"And David encouraged himself in the Lord his God."

Day Nine

Coping With Stress

Jesus was under constant pressure but he remained at peace under pressure. He was calm, at ease, never in a hurry, never uptight.

How did he do it? He based his life on sound principles of stress management. He kept his priorities in order. His number one priority was his relationship with his Father.

That's why no matter how busy he was Jesus took time to pray and spend time in God's presence.

"Very early in the morning, while it was still dark, Jesus got up, left the house and went off to a solitary place, where he prayed" (Mark 1:35 NIV).

(When was the last time you got up early to pray and read God's word?)

Prayer is a great stress reliever.

Let me ask you a question. If Jesus felt prayer was so important that he took time for it even when he was extremely busy, how much more do you and I need to pray?

"But those who wait on the LORD Shall renew their strength; They shall mount up with wings like eagles, They shall run and not be weary, They shall walk and not faint" (Isaiah 40:31 NKJV).

Day Ten

Hope in the Lord

"Be strong and take heart, all you who hope in the Lord" (Psalm 31:24 NIV).

Hope is a feeling that what is wanted will someday happen. It is desire accompanied by expectation. Despair is the opposite of hope. We are all tempted to despair from time to time, but God's word offers us hope.

Hope is what enables us to wait patiently for the fulfillment of God's promises.

"But if we hope for what we do not yet have, we wait for it patiently" (Romans 8:25; Romans 4:17-21; Psalm 27:13-14; Psalm 119:114, 147 NIV).

Hope enables us to praise God while we wait.

"But I will hope continually and will praise you yet more and more" (Psalm 71:14 NKJV).

Day Eleven

Hope in God

God is the true source of help, hope and happiness. If you rely on someone else to make you happy you are guaranteed to get hurt. You will be disappointed. Human beings have a tendency to let each other down – even when they don't intend to – even when they don't realize it.

Jeremiah says, *"Blessed is the man who trusts in the Lord, and whose hope is in the Lord"* (Jeremiah 17:7 NKJV).

This person is not so easily hurt and disappointed by people. His happiness does not depend on how others treat him. His expectations are in the Lord.

"He will be like a tree planted by the waters" (Jeremiah 17:8 TLV).

This is the secret of a fulfilled and fruitful life: "Get close to the river of life and put your roots down deep in God's word."

Hope in God, hope in His word, and no matter what happens in this world you will be able to say, "I am blessed."

Day Twelve

Another Chance

"Never be ashamed of trying and failing. Only those who never try, never fail. He who tries and fails is less a failure than he who doesn't try at all."

Everyone makes a mistake now and then. Most people fail at a few things in life. Many are still living with the regret of past mistakes. They are afraid to step out in faith to try something new because of past failures.

Pain from the past can be devastating. Someone reading this needs to take Paul's advice in Philippians 3:13, *"…I am bringing all my energies to bear on this one thing: Forgetting the past and looking forward to what lies ahead"* (LB).

Before you say, "I can't," say, "I'll try," then give it your best!

Vern McLellan says, "He who never makes a mistake works for the man who does."

"A man who refuses to admit his mistakes can never be successful. But if he confesses and forsakes them, he gets another chance" (Proverbs 28:13 TLB).

Day Thirteen

Problem or Possibility?

Today I want to encourage you to work on developing a positive attitude by faith.

I heard a great story about a little boy who was talking to himself as played ball alone in his back yard. "I'm the greatest ball player in the world," he said as he tossed baseball into the air, swung at it and missed. Undaunted he picked the ball up again, tossed it into the air and said, "I'm the greatest ball player in the neighborhood." He missed again. He paused for a moment, looked at his bat and ball, then threw the ball up again. "I'm the greatest baseball player who ever lived, "he exclaimed. He swung the bat hard and again missed the ball. "Wow!" he exclaimed, "What a pitcher!"

That's the kind of attitude that will make you a winner. That's the kind of attitude that will inspire you to get up, dust yourself off and try again after a failure or set back. That's the kind of attitude that will cause you take a risk to accomplish something for God.

Opportunities are seized by people who make the decision to go for it even though risk is involved.

Problems can be transformed into possibilities by faith. Obstacles can become opportunities.

Day Fourteen

Born to Win

We are born to win, but conditioned to lose. The negative forces at work in the world try to steal our victory in Christ. We need to remind one another that God wants us to be winners. He wants to help us.

"If God is for us who can be against us" (Romans 8:31 NKJV).

"In all these things we are more than conquerors (we are winners!) through him who loved us" (Romans 8:37 KJV).

Winners are ordinary people with extraordinary determination. The apostle Paul was that kind of person. In 1 Corinthians 9:26 he said, *"...so I run straight to the goal with purpose in every step. I fight to win. I'm not just shadow boxing or playing around"* (LB).

He wrote in Philippians 3:13-14, *"No, dear brothers, I am still not all I should be but I am binging all my energies to bear on this one thing: Forgetting the past and looking forward to what lies ahead, I strain to reach the end of the race and receive the prize for which God is calling us up to heaven because of what Jesus did for us"* (LB).

A winner isn't somebody who never fails or never falls. A winner is somebody who fails and tries again. A winner is often somebody who falls down nine times and gets up ten. So, "if at first you don't succeed go ahead and try it again!"

Day Fifteen

Things I Can Boldly Say

1. God will help me.

> *"So we may boldly say: The Lord is my helper; I will not fear. What can man do to me?"* (Hebrews 13:6 NKJV).

2. God will not fail me.

> *"Blessed be the Lord who has given rest to his people Israel according to all that he has promised. There has not failed one word of all his good promise..."* (1 Kings 8:56 NKJV).

3. God will defend me.

> *"But let all those rejoice who put their trust in You; Let them ever shout for joy, because You defend them; Let those also who love Your name Be joyful in You"* (Psalm 5:11).

4. God will deliver me.

> *"He shall call upon Me, and I will answer him; I will be with him in trouble; I will deliver him and honor him ..."* (Psalm 91:15 NKJV).

5. God will lead me to victory.

> *"Thanks be to God who always leads us in triumph in Christ..."* (2 Corinthians 2:14 NKJV).

Day Sixteen

Living With Eternal Perspective

What are the most valuable things in life? The things that will outlast life here on earth.

"Just one life will soon be past; Only what's done for Christ will last."

You can't take your money or possessions to heaven with you but you can help get people there. God is not searching for gold in the earth. He is looking for a family. He is searching for His lost children. That's why He continually challenges us to invest our lives in his kingdom. That's why He is looking for Christians with eternal perspective who will make investments of their time, energy and money to reach the lost.

"Don't store up treasures here on earth where they can erode away or be stolen. Store them in heaven where they will never lose their value…For where you treasure is there will your heart be also" (Matthew 6:19-21 LB and NKJV).

"Don't worry about things…Why be like the heathen? For they take pride in all these things and are deeply concerned about them…But you seek first the kingdom of God and His righteousness and all these things shall be added unto you" (Matthew 6:25, 31-33 LB and NKJV).

Day Seventeen

Don't Give Up

"And he spoke a parable unto them to this end, that men ought always to pray and not to faint" (Luke 18:1 KJ21).

Other translations render "not to faint" as "not to lose heart" or "not to give up".

"When He rose up from prayer, and had come to His disciples, He found them sleeping from sorrow. Then He said to them, "Why do you sleep? Rise and pray, lest you enter into temptation." (Luke 22:45-46 NKJV).

"Then he came and found them sleeping, and said to Peter, 'Simon are you sleeping? Could you not watch one hour?'" (Mark 14:37 NKJV)

"Again he went away and prayed, and spoke the same words" (Mark 14:39 NKJV).

"And when he had returned, he found them asleep again, for their eyes were heavy; and they did not know what to answer him" (Mark 14:40 NKJV).

Jesus told his disciples:

1. Pray so you won't lose heart.

2. Pray so you won't fall into temptation.

They responded by going to sleep while he prayed. When he returned he had two questions for them:

1. Why are you sleeping?

2. Couldn't you pray for one hour?

"Prayer is the most needed and the most neglected activity in the church today."

If you truly want God to move in your life, in your family, in your church, in you world, then you need to pray. You must pray.

Day Eighteen

Renewed Hope

"Master, we have toiled all night and have caught nothing" (Luke 5:5 NKJV).

Peter, James and John had fished all night with no success. They were fishermen by trade. They had failed to catch the fish that they needed to sell to pay their bills, to support their families.

They were exhausted and discouraged. Their boat was empty. Their nets were torn. They had worked hard, but had nothing to show for it. Can you imagine how they must have felt at that moment? Perhaps you have had similar experiences – maybe you are facing overwhelming problems right now.

Jesus came to Peter, James and John in the midst of their discouragement. His presence changed everything. He wants to do the same for you.

What did Jesus do for Peter? He gave him renewed hope. He got in his boat and told him to try it again.

Peter acted in faith at the Word of the Lord and caught a net breaking, boat sinking load. Are you at a point in your life where nothing but a miracle can help you? Then expect a miracle! God loves you as much as he loves Peter. Don't give up. Don't quit. Remember, "If the outlook is bad, try the uplook." Look up to God and expect Him to help you. He said He would and He keeps His promises.

"For the vision is yet for an appointed time; But at the end it will speak, and it will not lie. Though it tarries, wait for it; Because it will surely come, It will not tarry" (Habakkuk 2:3).

Day Nineteen

God Has Not Forgotten You

Psalm 37:4 says to, *"Delight yourself in the Lord and he will give you the desires of your heart."* God wants us to experience joy and pleasure in our fellowship with him.

Many Christians have temporarily lost their joy because of problems and pressures in the world. It is difficult to delight yourself in the Lord when you are disappointed, stressed out and burdened with worry. The Bible has a remedy for this condition.

1 Peter 5:7 says, *"Cast all your care on him; for he cares for you."* God hasn't forgotten you. He wants to help you find peace and joy again. He wants to deliver you from your worries and fears.

Your situation may be difficult but it is not impossible. God can help you. One thing is certain. You can never worry your way out of a problem. It takes faith to bring the power of God on the scene. These verses will strengthen your faith and help you believe God for deliverance and victory:

"Don't worry about whether you have enough food to eat or clothes to wear. For life consists of more than food and clothes... God will give you all you need from day to day if you make the kingdom of God your primary concern. So don't be afraid... For it gives your father great happiness to give you the kingdom" (from Luke 12:22-32 LB).

I want to encourage you to do two things. Cast your cares on God. Reach out to him in faith for the help you need.

If you will do this day after day – no matter what comes your way – it won't be long before you are delighting yourself in the Lord and experiencing joy in your salvation.

Day Twenty

If You Can Believe

The father of the demon possessed boy in Mark 9:17-27 (NKJV) said to Jesus, *"If you can do anything have compassion on us and help us"* (v. 22). You may know the story. The boy was delivered. I want you to know today that you have more faith than that boy's father had. He said, "if you can help us." You don't even need to ask that question. You know He can help you. If that boy's father with limited faith – actually a mixture of faith and unbelief – got help from God, you can, too.

Notice how Jesus answered him, *"If you can believe, all things are possible to him that believes"* (v. 23). The man immediately answered, *"Lord I believe; help my unbelief."* (v. 24) He was saying, "I believe and I don't believe." Most of us can relate to that. The thing I want you to notice is that Jesus didn't rebuke him for his unbelief. He encouraged his faith.

Don't be discouraged if your faith has faltered. Don't let an unsolved problem or an unmet need cause you to give up. Let it motivate you to reach out for stronger faith. There is an answer to your problem. There is help for you in time of need. Your situation is not impossible because, "all things are possible to the one who believes."

Day Twenty-One

Why You Need Problems

The problems and troubles of life are not always enemies. They can be friends that move us closer to God. Problems provide opportunities to exercise faith. It is true that problems can become possibilities by faith. Problems can be friends that help our prayer life. They cause us to be more dependent on God. Sometimes a problem we view as an obstacle is really a stepping stone to higher ground. Someone has said that "if we never had a problem we wouldn't know that God could solve them."

"Often the best friend a man ever has is not comfort, but the stimulus and challenge of an antagonistic environment to awaken the resistance of his slumbering soul." (Harry Emerson Fosdick)

"And now in obedience to the Holy Spirit I am going to Jerusalem, not knowing what will happen to me there. I only know that the Holy Spirit has warned me that prison and troubles wait for me. But none of these things move me; nor do I count my life dear to myself, so that I may finish my race with joy, and the ministry which I received from the Lord Jesus, to testify to the gospel of the grace of God." (The apostle Paul from Acts 20:22-24 NKJV and Good News Bibles.)

Day Twenty-Two

You Can Do It

"I can do all things through Christ who strengthens me" (Philippians 4:13 NKJV).

God will give grace and strength equal to the task. Nothing He sends – or allows – into our lives is greater than His abundant grace. Paul wrote in 1 Corinthians 10:13, *"No temptation (or test or trial) has overtaken you except such as is common to man; (others have problems, too) but God is faithful, who will not allow you to be tempted (or tested or tried) above what you are able to bear…"* (NKJV).

One of the ways you witness to unbelievers is by your attitude in the difficult times – during the trials of life, when you are in the trenches, when someone has hurt you, when things aren't going your way. If you find strength through your communion with Christ, and maintain an attitude of faith and victory in such times, the world will notice. Your life will convince some hell bound sinner that there is something to Christianity, after all.

Difficulties can be the occasion for the unlocking of larger resources in the unsearchable riches of Christ. Every difficulty can send you searching for a promise – a promise which will lead you to victory.

The world will notice when a Christian bears sorrow with hopeful courage, meets disappointment with faith, endures uncertainty with patience and responds to hurts and offenses with love. Difficult? Yes, but possible. Possible because the same love that nailed Jesus to the cross, and then lifted Him from the grave, is still alive and working in the heart of Christians today. We are *still "more than conquerors through Him that loved us"* (Romans 8:37 NKJV).

Day Twenty-Three

Rise to the Challenge

Christians are engaged in the greatest cause of all time – the evangelization of the world. The greatest business on earth is God's business. The highest responsibility ever given to mankind is the Great Commission:

"And Jesus came and spoke to them, saying, "All authority has been given to Me in heaven and on earth. Go therefore and make disciples of all the nations, baptizing them in the name of the Father and of the Son and of the Holy Spirit, teaching them to observe all things that I have commanded you…" (Matthew 28:18-20 NKJV).

We should feel honored to be invited by Jesus to become members of God's family on earth – the church. You were personally invited by God to join an organization which was planned in heaven and established on earth by Jesus Christ.

We should feel privileged to be commissioned as ambassadors, His representatives on earth entrusted with the most powerful message of the ages – the gospel – the Good News of God's love for mankind.

You have been called with a high and holy calling. You have been entrusted with great responsibility. I dare you to rise to the challenge and "be the best you can be" for God. He deserves the best you can offer.

"I beseech you therefore brethren by the mercies of God, that you present your bodies a living sacrifice, holy, acceptable to God, which is your reasonable service" (Romans 12:1 NKJV).

Day Twenty-Four

Triumph in Trouble

A common misconception of the ideal Christian life is that it means deliverance from trouble. Actually, God has promised deliverance "in trouble", not always "from trouble". Joseph in the pit (Genesis 37) and Daniel in the den (Daniel 3) are good examples of this truth. Jesus never promised escape from the troubles of life. *"...in the world you will have tribulation: but be of good cheer; I have overcome the world"* (John 16:33 NKJV).

This is good news for the child of God in troubling times. You may have troubles but trouble need not triumph over you. You share in Christ's victory. Jesus tells us not to be surprised when troubles come. He doesn't want us to be discouraged during times of struggle and strain. He wants us to receive strength for the struggle and to be of good cheer – even in the midst of trouble.

You can rejoice knowing that with God's help you will outlast your troubles. Someday you will be able to look back and wonder why you were so worried, if you learn that: *"God is our refuge and strength, a very present help in trouble"* (Psalm 46:1 NKJV).

Day Twenty-Five

Receiving the Promise

"We do not want you to become lazy, but to be like those who believe and are patient, and so receive what God has promised" (Hebrews 6:12 GNT).

In the next verses Paul gives Abraham as an example of this and says in verse 15, *"Abraham was patient, and so he received what God had promised."*

Abraham made some mistakes during the waiting phase. He struggled with unbelief. He got discouraged. He actually became impatient, got tired of waiting for God to fulfill His promise and took matters into his own hands. The birth of Ishmael, the progenitor of the Islamic Arab nations, was the result. These nations have opposed Christianity throughout history.

Isn't it interesting to see that in the New Testament God had nothing negative to say about Abraham? None of his mistakes are mentioned. None of his faults are listed. He is God's man of faith who didn't give up when the going got tough. Let's follow his example.

"But we do not belong to those who shrink back and are destroyed, but to those who have faith and are saved" (Hebrews 10:39 NIV).

"So do not throw away your confidence; it will be richly rewarded. You need to persevere so that when you have done the will of God you will receive what He has promised" (Hebrews 10:35-36 NIV).

Day Twenty-Six

Hope in God

Webster defines "depress" like this: "to press down; to cause to sink to a lower position; to lessen the activity or strength of." Characteristics of depression include sadness, inactivity, difficulty in thinking and concentration and feeling of dejection and hopelessness.

Everybody, including dedicated Christian, experiences bouts with depression. It can begin with disappointment and then move through a cycle of discouragement, despondency and finally despair. Rejection, loneliness and hurts from troubled or broken relationships can lead to depression.

So, how can you overcome depression – especially when you are lonely or hurting? Become Christ-centered, not self-centered. The key to victory over depression is not a change in circumstances but a change in you. Happiness does not depend on favorable circumstances but on your relationship with God. The prophet Habakkuk had every right to be depressed over negative circumstances in his life but look what he says in Habakkuk 3:17-18, (Living Bible)

"Even though the fig trees are all destroyed, and there is neither blossom left nor fruit, and though the olive crops fail, and the fields lie barren; even if the flocks die in the fields and the cattle barns are empty, yet I will rejoice in the Lord; I will be happy in the God of my salvation."

If you are depressed today do what David did; hope in God. With his help you can overcome depression.

"Why are you cast down, O my soul? And why are you disquieted within me? Hope in God; for I shall yet praise Him, the help of my countenance and my God" (Psalm 42:11 NKJV).

Day Twenty-Seven

Rise Above It

I want to encourage you to rejoice in the spirit even if you don't feel like it! Don't cooperate with the devil. He wants you to think, "I'm so worn out and discouraged I don't feel like praising God." If that's where you are today I challenge you to rise above your feelings by faith and praise God enthusiastically. What do you have to lose! Here's something to rejoice about:

"I will greatly rejoice in the Lord, my soul shall be joyful in my God; for He has clothed me with the garments of salvation, He has covered me with the robe of righteousness…" (Isaiah 61:10 NKJV).

You may have struggles. You may have needs. You may have problems. But you still have reason to rejoice because God has dressed you up in the garments of salvation and covered you with a robe of righteousness.

Remember what the prophet Habakkuk said to the farmers in Israel in hard times:

"Even though the fig trees are all destroyed…and though the olive crops all fail, and the fields be barren; even if the flocks die in the fields and the cattle barns are empty," (and you thought you had problems!) *"Yet will I rejoice in the Lord; I will be happy in the God of my salvation"* (Habakkuk 3:17-18 TLB).

Here's what I want you to get hold of: Habakkuk couldn't be happy over his circumstances, so he decided to be happy in his God.

Day Twenty-Eight

Fight the Good Fight

Everywhere I look I see people who are facing serious circumstances. Many are facing hopelessness. Everything has come crashing down around them.

Hopelessness is a spirit which brings heaviness or depression. It will steal your faith, peace and joy. It comes when the fight of faith is almost gone from your heart. It comes when your power to resist is greatly diminished. But you must fight it! Hopelessness won't leave until you force it to leave.

How can you overcome it?

1. First, you must stop fretting and start fighting. *"Fight the good fight of faith"* (1 Timothy 6:12 NKJV).

2. Second, you must stop doubting and start believing. *"Abraham against hope believed into hope... he staggered not at the promise of God through unbelief; but was strong in faith giving glory to God"* (Romans 4:18, 20 WYC and KJV).

3. Third, you must stop complaining and start rejoicing (even if you don't feel like it).

The Bible says Jesus will, *"give beauty for ashes, the oil of joy for mourning, the garment of praise for the spirit of heaviness..."* (Isaiah 61:3 NKJV).

The road out of the valley of hopelessness begins at the point where you put on praise by faith and rejoice in God even though you can't rejoice in your circumstances.

Day Twenty-Nine

All Out for God

"Enoch walked with God" (Genesis 5:24 NKJV).

The test of a man's character is not what he does in the exceptional moments of life, but what he does in the ordinary times. A man's heart is often revealed by his attitude toward the ordinary things, the daily duties of life carried out when there is no crowd looking on. God is looking for such men, men of responsibility, faithful men who will seek Him, serve Him, draw near to Him.

Enoch was such a man. He got in step with God. He enjoyed intimacy, personal union with God. He lived in the wonderful atmosphere of God's presence. He breathed the fresh air of heaven. The life of God flowed through him. Enoch was all out for God. He would have none of the apathetic on again, off again experience common to many of God's people. He knew nothing of half hearted commitment.

When people saw Enoch they didn't say there's a man who goes to church on Sunday; they didn't say he's a good guy; they said, there's Enoch, the man who walks with God.

How do people identify you? I challenge you to get serious about living for God. Make it your goal to become known as a man or woman who walks with God.

"Then Jesus spoke to them again, saying, "I am the light of the world. He who follows Me shall not walk in darkness, but have the light of life"" (John 8:12).

Day Thirty

A Few Faithful Men

"The greatest ability is dependability."

God looks for men and women who will serve Him faithfully in every generation. He looks for dependable disciples – followers He can count on. Have you decided to make faithfulness a priority in your Christian life? Can God count on you?

There always seems to be a shortage of faithful men.

"Most men will proclaim each his own goodness, but who can find a faithful man?" (Proverbs 20:6 NKJV)

Jesus had a lot to say about the importance of faithfulness. He promised to bless those who faithfully served him. Are you a wise and faithful servant of the Lord? *"..Blessings on you if I return and find you faithfully doing your work"* (Matthew 24:45 LB).

God is looking for a few faithful men and women. Will you be one of them?

Day Thirty-One

Grace for the Humble

It is interesting that Jesus talked about both humility and hell in Mark 9:33-50. But when you think about it, humility is the reason Jesus is exalted in heaven and pride is why Satan was cast out of heaven.

Humility is produced by love. It is the grace of character which enables us to follow Jesus' example and give ourselves in service to others. Those who humble themselves and serve in the kingdom of God will one day be richly rewarded. Humility will exalt you. Pride will bring you low.

"But He gives more grace…God resists the proud, but gives grace to the humble…Humble yourselves in the sight of the Lord and He shall lift you up" (James 4:6, 10 NKJV).

"Let Christ Jesus be your example as to what your attitude should be…having become a man He humbled Himself…That is why God has now lifted Him so high…and that is why, in the end, every tongue shall confess that Jesus Christ is Lord…" (Philippians 2:5-11 Phillips).

Day Thirty-Two

Beating Bitterness

Hebrews 12:15 in the Good News Bible (GNT) says, *"Guard against turning back from the grace of God. Let no one become like a bitter plant that grows up and causes many troubles with its poison."*

Bitterness will poison your spirit. It will trouble and torment you. It can result from a wrong reaction to real or imagined ill-treatment. It can develop when you are hurt or offended or when you pick up someone else's offense. Picking up someone else's offense happens when you become bitter toward a person who has hurt someone you love.

It is not easy to live free of bitterness. It is difficult to forgive and release people who have hurt you -- difficult but possible. Hebrews 12:15 gives the key. *"Guard against turning back from the grace of God."* Grace can help you forgive people who have wronged and hurt you, even though they don't deserve your forgiveness. Sometimes it is humanly impossible to forgive; the wound is too deep. But grace can give you supernatural strength to do what is humanly impossible. You forgive others even though they don't deserve it because God forgave you.

Here's where to start. If you feel that you can't forgive and release someone, honestly tell God how you feel. Ask Him to help you to become willing to forgive. Then pray for grace to do what you know you need to do. As you forgive, grace will begin the healing process in your heart. You will be on the road to recovery.

"Get rid of all bitterness and anger. No more shouting or insults, no more hateful feelings of any sort. Instead, be kind and tender-hearted to one another, and forgive one another, as God has forgiven you through Christ" (Ephesians 4:31-32 Good News).

Day Thirty-Three

Hungry and Thirsty

"Blessed are those who hunger and thirst for righteousness for they shall be satisfied" (Matthew 5:6 ESV).

Appetite is one of the signs of health. When you are sick your appetite often decreases. Consequently, you lose strength.

The same is true spiritually. A healthy Christian has an appetite for the things of God. If you are in good shape spiritually you will desire God's word, worship and prayer.

Work and exercise increase appetite and build strength. Again, the same is true spiritually. The more you exercise yourself in the things of God the more you will desire to read the Bible, pray and worship.

What does your spiritual appetite tell you? Are you spiritually healthy? Little or no appetite indicates you are sick. You can recover though – if you want to. The Bible is not only spiritual food for the hungry; it is medicine for the sick.

"My son, give attention to my words; Incline your ear to my sayings. Do not let them depart from your eyes; Keep them in the midst of your heart; For they are life to those who find them, And health to all their flesh" (Proverbs 4:20-22 NKJV).

Day Thirty-Four

Partners With God

"For we are God's fellow workers…" (1 Corinthians 3:9 NKJV).

God has given us the privilege of entering into partnership with Him through the covenant He has established with those who respond to Him in faith.

We are engaged in the most important business in the world. We are here on business for the King.

We are involved in the greatest cause of all time – evangelism. We are working together with God to fulfill the Great Commission.

If we move in faith and cooperate with God, I know we can impact our culture through the power of the Spirit.

The following little story puts our partnership in perspective:

"We might feel like the little mouse who had to cross a bridge over a deep ravine in the jungle. He was afraid to walk across so he climbed up on a big elephant's head. As the little mouse and the elephant crossed the bridge it really shook and swayed. When they got to the other side the little mouse proudly exclaimed, "Boy, we really shook that bridge, didn't we!"

Day Thirty-Five

Be Filled With The Spirit

"And be not drunk with wine…But be filled with the Spirit; speaking to yourselves in psalms and hymns and spiritual songs, singing and making melody in your heart to the Lord; giving thanks always to God the Father in the name of our Lord Jesus Christ" (Ephesians 5:18-20 KJV).

I want to encourage you to seek a fresh infilling of the Holy Spirit. There are evil, supernatural forces at work in our world, and we need the supernatural power of God to combat them. Satan wants to steal your faith, your joy, and your strength. He wants you to become a discouraged, apathetic Christian who is devoid of the power of God.

Jesus said evil would increase just before His second coming, and that because of the influence of evil the love of many would grow cold, but that those who endure to the end would be saved (Matthew 24:12-13). To endure to the end we need God's power, we need to be filled with the Holy Spirit. You don't have to join the growing number of defeated, apathetic Christians. You don't have to become a spiritual casualty. It is possible, even in difficult and evil times, to live a victorious Christian life. How? Be filled with the Spirit.

"…He who is in you is greater than He who is in the world" (1 John 4:4 NKJV).

Day Thirty-Six

Breathe On Us

We must have a spiritual breakthrough in the church which will deliver us from complacency, and propel us forward with a deep love for God burning in our hearts. We need a fresh anointing of the Holy Spirit. We need the Holy Spirit to breathe upon us as He did the early church.

Hunger for God – a longing, a yearning to experience His faithfulness, precedes outpourings of the Spirit. God is not hiding. He told us how to find Him.

"And you will seek Me, and find Me, when you search for Me with all your heart" (Jeremiah 29:13 NKJV).

"Blessed are those who hunger and thirst after righteousness, for they shall be filled" (Matthew 5:6 NKJV).

That's what happened to the church on the Day of Pentecost. A few believers were hungry for God – so hungry they gathered in the Upper Room to pray.

"These all continued with one accord in prayer…"; "And they were all filled with the Holy Spirit and began to speak with other tongues…" (Acts 1:14 and 2:4 NKJV).

The mighty rushing wind of Pentecost blew upon a praying church. Prayer went up. Power came down. The formula hasn't changed. If we want the power of God, it's time to stop talking about it and start praying for it.

Day Thirty-Seven

The Power of Words

"You are snared with the words of your mouth; you are taken with the words of your mouth" (Proverbs 6:2 NKJV).

"A wholesome tongue is a tree of life: but perverseness therein is a breach in the spirit" (Proverbs 15:4 KJV).

"Death and life are in the power of the tongue: and they that love it shall eat the fruit thereof" (Proverbs 18:21 KJV).

Perhaps you know someone who can supposedly "talk his way out of anything." You might also know someone who has a real knack for talking his way into things – someone whose careless use of words constantly causes problems or gets him into unpleasant predicaments. These are just two practical examples of the power of words in everyday situations.

It is important for Christians who want to experience success and victory to train themselves to speak positive words of faith. The words you speak are the fruit of your spirit. Words can either build up or tear down; they can cause a blessing or a curse; they can deliver or condemn; they can heal or hurt. Just how serious is this issue for Christians? Here's what Jesus says, *"A good man out of the good treasure of his heart brings forth good things, and an evil man out of the evil treasure brings forth evil things"* (Matthew 12:35 NKJV).

Jesus is saying that the heart is like a "bank" where you can store treasure which can be drawn out later by the spoken word. The best way to store up good treasure is to hide God's word in your heart.

Jesus goes on to say, *"But I say to you that for every idle word men may speak, they will give account of it in the Day of Judgment. For by your words you will be justified, and by your words you will be condemned"* (Matthew 12:36-37 NKJV).

Day Thirty-Eight

Rebounding from Failure

"But Peter standing up with the eleven raised his voice, and said to them…hearken to my words" (Acts 2:14 NKJV).

Peter rebounded from failure over and over again. He was ready to quit the ministry and go fishing after the crucifixion. He was so disappointed in himself for denying Jesus, he didn't have the heart to continue. But Jesus went looking for him. He found him, forgave him, and encouraged him to go on. Peter was transformed. After being baptized with the Holy Spirit on the Day of Pentecost, Peter experienced incredible success in ministry. He is an example for everyone who truly wants to recover from setbacks, walk away from failures of the past, take hold of the grace of God, and move forward toward victory and success in life.

One of my favorite stories from Peter's life is from Luke 5:1-11 (NKJV). He was an accomplished fisherman, but he had worked all night without catching a single fish. He was tired, frustrated and discouraged when Jesus came along. After using Peter's boat to deliver a sermon to a crowd on the beach, Jesus told Peter to launch out into deep water and let down the nets for a catch. Good fishermen knew that you didn't catch much In those waters during the day. But Peter did what Jesus told him to do…*"nevertheless at Thy word I will let down the nets…"*.

Here are the lessons we need to learn from Peter's failure. He did everything he knew to do but had no success. He worked until all hope was gone. He was tired, ready to quit and go home. But two things turned Peter's failure into a stepping stone to success: the presence of the Lord and the word of the Lord. Jesus got in Peter's boat. Jesus told him what to do. Peter listened and obeyed. The result was – "a net breaking, boat sinking load." Jesus can do the same for you. He can turn your failure into a stepping stone to success.

Day Thirty-Nine

Regroup and Recover

"Do not remember the former things, nor consider the things of old. Behold, I will do a new thing…" (Isaiah 43:18-19 NKJV).

Everyone has some painful memories and painful experiences in their past. Most people have experienced setbacks at some time. The tragedy is not that most people experience setbacks, defeats or failures; the tragedy is that some never bounce back – they never recover. They spend their present dwelling on the past. Consequently, their future looks bleak because they drag the past into it.

There is a better way. It is possible to regroup and recover. You can experience healing and deliverance from the pain of your past. If you experienced financial reversal, you can bounce back with God's help. If you experienced failure in a relationship, you can find grace to forgive and move on with your life.

With God's help you can overcome the unbelief which has robbed you of hope. God's word can give you strength and faith: to stop dwelling on old mistakes and start looking for new opportunities; to stop dwelling on past problems and start searching for new possibilities; to move away from past defeats and press forward to new victories.

You can continue reliving and rehearsing the regrets of the past, or you can regroup and move forward with an attitude of faith and victory. It's your choice.

Recovery begins when you renew your commitment to God, and begin a new journey of faith that will take you out of the wilderness of unbelief.

"...Be strong and of good courage; be not afraid, neither be dismayed: for the Lord your God is with you wherever you go" (Joshua 1:9 NKJV).

Day Forty

The Creative Power of Words

"Let us hold fast the profession of our hope without wavering, for He who promised is faithful" (Hebrews 10:36 NKJV).

It can be difficult to maintain a good confession and a positive attitude of faith when things are going wrong, or when things are going right but too slowly. It can be particularly difficult during a long period of little or no progress. Sometimes, when there seems to be no forward progress, all we can do is stand in faith (see Ephesians 6:10-12).

What we say and do during the slow-moving phase of little progress is extremely important. Without a positive confession of faith we won't be prepared to move on when the stand-waiting phase is over.

The words you speak will work for you or they will work against you. Words have creative power. Your life will go out after your words. Your life will follow your words. Here's another way to say it: "You lay the tracks you will travel on by the words you speak."

Have you experienced delay, frustration, failure? Are you experiencing them now? What should you do?

"Hold fast the profession of your hope."

Believe that with God's help you will overcome and experience success. Act like you believe it. Talk like you believe it. Your words will build a highway into the future. "You" listen to every word "you" speak. "You" can talk "you" into an attitude of victory or defeat.

Let's begin building a highway to success right now. If you have passed through -- or are passing through --tough times, start talking your way out of them right now by speaking God's Word in faith.

Are there some things against you? Answer them with Romans 8:31 (KJV) - *"If God be for us who can be against us?"*

Do you think you are a failure? God doesn't. "Nay, in all these things we are more than conquerors through him that loved us" (Romans 8:37 KJV). Simple? Yes. So simple that it works!

The devil can't keep a Christian down if he will:

1) Hold on to faith.

2) Speak God's Word in faith.

3) Act on God's Word in faith.

Day Forty-One

Confession and Faith

If we believe something from God's word we must act like we believe it and talk like we believe it. The word of faith must be in our mouths as well as in our hearts (Romans 10:8-10).

Confession is:
1) Affirming something we believe, and
2) Testifying to something we know.

What we say with our mouths reveals what we believe in our hearts. What we believe is influenced by what we think. Our minds must be renewed by the word of God before we can experience right thinking and right believing (Romans 12:2).

When we read or listen to God's word, faith is produced in our hearts. Confessing words of faith brings results. The keys to victory are: 1) "right" thinking; 2) "right" believing; and 3) "right" confessing. To experience victory we must: 1) learn what the Bible promises and think about it; 2) believe what the Bible says; 3) confess what the Bible says. It's simple but effective.

Here are some examples of confessing God's word in faith: *"'Fear not for I am with you; be not dismayed, for I am your God. I will strengthen you, yes I will help you, I will uphold you with My righteous right hand'"* (Isaiah 41:10 NKJV).

When you are struggling, discouraged or fearful read verses like this and then confess: God is with me; God will strengthen me; God will help me; God will uphold me. Do it enough and you will convince yourself it's true.

Here's a verse for times when you feel unloved, insecure and a little mentally scattered: *"For God has not given us a spirit of fear, but of power and of love and of a sound mind"* (2 Timothy 1:7 NKJV).

The Bible is filled with positive promises like these to help you in times of struggle. Learn them, believe them, confess them, and in time victory will come your way.

Day Forty-Two

The Joy of His Presence

"When I said, 'My foot is slipping,' Your unfailing love, Lord, supported me. When anxiety was great within me, Your consolation brought me joy" (Psalm 94:18-19 NIV).

God is compassionate and understanding. He knows our weaknesses, but He does not reject us because of them. He has wrath against sin, but He extends mercy to repentant sinners. The Psalmist was slipping, about to fall, but when he humbled himself and acknowledged his need, God came to help. *"Your love, Lord, supported me."* When you have lost control, when your predicament is beyond human remedy, God does not expect you to save yourself; He does expect you to humbly reach out to Him for help and strength.

The writer goes on to say, *"When anxiety was great within me, your consolation brought me joy."* You don't have to wait for your problems to go away – for your circumstances to change – before you can experience joy. God can flood your soul with joy in the midst of your struggle. You can know the joy of His presence – and the strength it brings – if you humbly cry out to Him in your time of need.

"I will be glad and rejoice in your mercy, for You have considered my trouble; You have known my soul in adversities" (Psalm 31:7 NKJV).

Day Forty-Three

Yes We Can!

"Then Caleb quieted the people before Moses, and said, "Let us go up at once and take possession, for we are well able to overcome it." But the men who had gone up with him said, "We are not able to go up against the people, for they are stronger than we."" (Numbers 13:30-31 NKJV).

Two reports – one negative and one positive; two spirits – a spirit of faith and a spirit of unbelief. Which prevailed? Unfortunately the negative report and the spirit of unbelief carried the day. What happened to those who brought the negative report? They perished in the wilderness. What happened to those who brought the positive report? They entered the Promised Land.

Here we see two spirits fighting for influence over the people of God. Because it is the tendency of human nature to believe an evil report, the negative spirit of unbelief prevailed. Try to picture what happened here. The children of Israel have finally reached the border of the Promised Land. They are poised to cross over the Jordan in faith, but the evil report causes great turmoil. In just a matter of moments they have turned on Moses and are ready to go back to the wilderness. Yesterday Moses was the anointed leader who brought them out of Egypt to the border of the Promised Land. Now he is the misguided prophet who brought them to this place for certain destruction.

The children of Israel became the "yes, but crowd". "Yes, the land is a rich land, but; yes, Moses is an anointed leader, but…" etc., etc. The influence of the evil report caused them to doubt. Satan had them set up for frustration and failure.

They went back to the wilderness.

Fortunately the story doesn't end there. The "no we can't crowd" perished in the wilderness but the "yes we can crowd" finally won. Joshua and Caleb eventually led a victorious, faith-filled, younger generation into the Promised Land. The "yes, but crowd" was silenced. The "we can do it crowd" won the final round.

"...Truly the Lord has delivered all the land into our hands ..." (Joshua 2:24 NKJV). Yes we can!

Day Forty-Four

Unshakable Faith

"What then shall we then say to these things?" (Romans 8:31 NKJV)

What things? *"…tribulation, distress, persecution, lack, peril, etc…"* (Romans 8:35)

"If God be for us, who can be against us? Nay, in all these things we are more than conquerors through him that loved us" (Romans 8:31 and 8:37 KJV).

"But none of these things move me, neither count I my life dear to myself, so that I might finish my course with joy, and the ministry, which I have received of the Lord Jesus, to testify the gospel of the grace of God" (Acts 20:24 NKJV).

Paul had an immovable, unshakable faith. Pressure and struggle didn't stop him because he knew that the moment we get anything from the Lord worth contending for, the powers of darkness will attack and endeavor to steal it from us. At those moments, we need to stand strong in faith and say with Paul "none of these things move me." When spiritual enemies engage us at the threshold of spiritual progress, let us welcome the battle and proclaim blessing and victory. Power is developed by resistance. It takes friction to produce electricity. Tribulation can be the pathway to triumph. Success comes to those who persevere under pressure.

The low road of Christianity is the negative way of doubt and fear. The high road is the positive path of faith and courage. The Christian who, in the midst of struggle and trial, keeps his head, holds onto his faith, and stays his course through the storm, is destined to win. Faith will transform the raging sea which threatens to overcome into a friend which carries the believer forward to greater blessing. The winds of adversity which once hindered spiritual progress will be transformed into the winds of victory which carry the believer to new heights of faith. Some Christians lower the lifeboats and jump ship at the slightest hint of a storm. Others panic and act as if a small storm were a hurricane. This "making a mountain out of a molehill" mentality will always lead to frustration, weakness and defeat. It is the Christian who traverses the troubled sea with faith in his heart and God's word in his mouth who triumphs. He will be stronger and better for having made the journey.

"Nay, in all these things we are more than conquerors..."

Day Forty-Five

The Power of the Spirit

"But you will receive power when the Holy Spirit comes upon you. And you will be my witnesses, telling people about me everywhere—in Jerusalem, throughout Judea, in Samaria, and to the ends of the earth" (Acts 1:8 NLT).

The Holy Spirit gives us power! We need the power of God to do the work of God. Too many churches are running on man's machinery, not God's power. The Holy Spirit not only gives us power to witness – He gives us power to live a victorious life. Through the Holy Spirit we can have victory even in the midst of trying circumstances. Immediately after Jesus received the blessing of the baptism, He was driven by the Spirit into the wilderness. What happened there? He was tempted of the devil. He waged spiritual warfare. He won the battle in the power of the Spirit. You may find yourself in the greatest spiritual battle of your life after receiving the baptism in the Holy Spirit - but now you have a greater power with which to fight.   Acts 1:8 says specifically that we will receive power to be witnesses. What a wonderful privilege to be called and empowered by God to go forth to share the glorious gospel.   As Christians, the power of God is available to us. It remains for us to reach out and receive it by faith.

Day Forty-Six

The Blessing of Knowing God

"But let him who glories, glory in this, that he understands and knows Me, that I am the Lord who exercises loving kindness, judgment, and righteousness, in the earth: for in these things I delight, says the Lord" (Jeremiah 9:24 NKJV).

Have you stopped to consider lately how blessed you are to know the living God? This verse tells us why we can rejoice:

1) He is the Lord. We are in a relationship with the Creator and Ruler of the universe. A personal relationship with Him gives us access to "Heaven's White House," the control center of the universe.

2) He is loving and kind. Most of the world's population has a distorted perception of God. He is not perceived to be a God of love but an angry God who pours out His wrath if not appeased. Most people live with an unholy, unhealthy fear of God. You are blessed to know that He is a God of love, mercy and grace.

3) He is a righteous God who judges fairly. God is righteous in all His ways and fair in all His dealings with people. As a believer, you are blessed, not only by knowing He is righteous, but by experiencing His righteousness. The righteousness of God demands judgment against sin. But His loving kindness found a way to extend mercy to all who would receive Him.

I want to close with a verse from the New Testament which gives us more reason to glory (rejoice) that we know the living God: "For He made Him who knew no sin to be sin for us, that we might become the righteousness of God in Him" (2 Corinthians 5:21 NKJV).

What a deal! Let's spend some time rejoicing that we know God and that we are righteous in His sight.

Day Forty-Seven

Delivered and Blessed

When you are in a terrible struggle against the forces of evil it is important to know it is God's will for you to be delivered from evil. Jesus prayed in John 17:15, *"I do not pray that you should take them out of the world, but that you should keep them from the evil one"* (NKJV). We know that we will be free from the influence of evil in heaven, but this prayer is not about heaven. Jesus prayed that God would protect us, deliver us, from Satan's evil power on earth.

Jesus taught us to pray, *"lead us not into temptation, but deliver us from evil"* in Matthew 6:13 (KJV). Sin brought us under the bondage of the evil ruler of darkness. All the pain trouble and misery in the world stems from the curse of sin and the evil brought about by sin. Jesus not only prayed that we would be delivered from evil, he paid the price so we could be. *"Christ has redeemed us from the curse of the law, having become a curse for us (for it is written, "Cursed is everyone who hangs on a tree")"* (Galatians 3"13 NKJV). With His own blood Jesus redeemed us, and paid for our past failure and sin. Now, by God's power you can be set free from the pain and mistakes of the past. You can receive forgiveness, cleansing, and freedom from past sins. Don't be a prisoner of the past. Open your heart to receive God's love, healing and forgiveness. Cut the cords that bind you to painful experiences from years gone by. Jesus can set you free from the curse of haunting memories from the past.

Now claim your deliverance from the curse of past and present evil, and move forward into a future of blessing by faith. Jesus not only provided for your deliverance, He opened the way for you to be blessed of *God "that the blessing of Abraham might come upon the Gentiles in Christ Jesus, that we might receive the promise of the Spirit through faith"* (Galatians 3:14 NKJV). When God delivers you from one thing, he brings you into another. You were delivered from the darkness and brought into the light; you were delivered from sin and brought into righteousness; you were delivered from bondage and brought into liberty; you were delivered from defeat and brought into victory; you were delivered from cursing and brought into blessing.

It's time to take a stand and declare, "I am blessed of God."

"So then those who are of faith are blessed with believing Abraham" (Galatians 3:9 NKJV).

"And now that we are Christ's we are the true descendents of Abraham, and all of God's promises to him belong to us (we are heirs of the promised blessings)" (Galatians 3:29 LB).

Day Forty-Eight

Halfway There and Tired

Why do people get discouraged? The primary reason is often fatigue. When Nehemiah inquired why the work on the wall around Jerusalem had come to a standstill, the response was, "The strength of the laborers is giving out." They had worked a long time without a break; they were worn out – physically and emotionally exhausted.

It is interesting to notice when fatigue and discouragement overcame them. *"So we built the wall, and the entire wall was joined together up to half its height, for the people had a mind to work"* (Nehemiah 4:6 NKJV). Shortly after the halfway point these words were spoken: *"Meanwhile, the people in Judah said, 'The strength of the laborers is giving out, and there is so much rubble that we cannot rebuild the wall'"* (v. 10-12 NIV). Halfway through, they were not only feeling tired and discouraged, but overwhelmed by the amount of work still before them – "there is so much rubble that we cannot rebuild the wall." The task seems harder, the problems loom larger, when fatigue and discouragement come over you.

Like many dedicated Christians, I have sometimes mistakenly assumed that my struggle against discouragement has been a spiritual problem. While praying more, getting into God's word, or renewing commitment can help, the problem is often more physical and emotional than spiritual. Rest, relaxation and recreation can often be the best medicine for discouragement.

Are you halfway there and tired? Don't condemn yourself for not being spiritual enough. Maybe you just need a rest. It's ok to take a break at half-time. And until you can take the extended vacation you probably need, remember that God can help you. He is your refuge and strength. You can retreat into His presence and find rest for your soul.

"He gives power to the weak, and to those who have no might He increases strength…those who wait upon the Lord shall renew their strength; they shall mount up with wings like eagles…" (Isaiah 40:29, 31 NKJV).

Day Forty-Nine

The Person God Blesses

"Blessed is the man who fears the Lord, who delights greatly in His commandments…He will not be afraid of evil tidings; his heart is steadfast, trusting in the Lord" (Psalm 112:1, 7 NKJV).

I wish space would allow us to print this entire Psalm here. It is filled with wonderful promises to the righteous: blessing on descendants, prosperity, light in the darkness, honor, victory are all promised to the man (or woman) this psalm describes.

These are all blessings you can claim in faith if you "fear the Lord and delight greatly in His commands."

Those who delight greatly in His commands love God's word – love to read it, hear it, and do it. Those who fear the Lord worship Him with holy reverence – in spirit and in truth. The cry of their heart is, *"Let the words of my mouth, and the meditation of my heart, be acceptable in Your sight, O Lord, my strength and my Redeemer"* (Psalm 19:14 NKJV).

Day Fifty

The Person God Blesses (Part 2)

"Blessed is the man who walks not in the counsel of the ungodly…But his delight is in the law of the Lord; and in His law he meditates day and night" (Psalm 1:1-2 NKJV).

We saw yesterday in Psalm 112 that the person who loves God's word is blessed. This is not only the blessing sovereignly bestowed by the Lord, but the blessing that comes as a result of loving and following God's word.

"Blessed are they that keep His testimonies, and that seek Him with their whole heart" (Psalm 119:2 KJV).

David knew that the way of blessing was in loving and following the word of the Lord. It is futile to claim, or to expect God's blessing, apart from a commitment to obey His word. That's why David went on to pray, *"With my whole heart I have sought you, Oh, let me not wander from your commandments"* (Psalm 119:10 NKJV).

God called David *"a man after My own heart"* (Acts 13:22 NKJV). Psalm 119 helps us understand the intimacy David experienced with the Lord. It is filled with statements expressing David's delight in and love for God's word.

"I will delight myself in Your commandments, which I love. Oh, how I love Your law! It is my meditation all the day" (vs. 47 and 97 NKJV).

"How sweet are Thy words to my taste! Yea, sweeter than honey to my mouth" (vs. 103 KJV).

"...my heart stands in awe of Your word" (vs. 161 NKJV).

"My soul has kept Your testimonies, and I love them exceedingly" (vs. 167 NKJV).

Will you join me in praying, "God help us to love Your word as David loved Your word."

Day Fifty-One

Be A Doer of the Word

"Now the Spirit speaketh expressly, that in the latter times some shall depart from the faith, giving heed to seducing spirits, and doctrines of devils" (1Timothy 4:1 KJV).

"…some in the church will turn away from Christ and become eager followers of teachers with devil inspired ideas" (Living Bible paraphrase).

Paul repeatedly warned against deception. His warnings have never been more relevant, or more necessary, than they are today. He described some additional characteristics of the last days in 2 Timothy.

"But understand this, that in the last days there will set in perilous times of great stress and trouble – hard to deal with and hard to bear…In fact, evil men and false teachers will become worse and worse, deceiving many, they themselves having been deceived by Satan…For there is going to come a time when people won't listen to the truth, but will go around looking for teachers who will tell them just what they want to hear. They won't listen to what the Bible says but will blithely follow their own misguided ideas" (2 Timothy 3:1, 13, 4:3, 4 LB and Amp).

If you want to avoid being numbered among the deceived, I have good news for you; the Bible clearly explains how a person can escape deception.

"The whole Bible was given to us by inspiration from God and is useful to teach us what is true and to make us realize what is wrong in our lives; it straightens us out and helps us

do what is right" (2 Timothy 3:16 LB).

The greatest safeguard against deception is to learn and apply the word of God.

"But be doers of the Word, and not hearers only, deceiving yourselves" (James 1:22 NKJV).

"Study to show yourself approved unto God, a worker who does not need to be ashamed, rightly dividing the word of truth" (2 Timothy 2:15 MEV).

Day Fifty-Two

Making The Right Choices

Making your life count begins with making the right choices. The Christian who makes right choices must first develop godly values and establish scriptural priorities. Sometimes the right choice is the difficult choice. This is demonstrated in the life of Moses. His godly choices resulted in temporary hardship, but ultimately in eternal reward.

"By faith Moses, when he became of age, refused to be called the son of Pharoh's daughter, choosing rather to suffer affliction with the people of God than to enjoy the passing pleasures of sin, esteeming the reproach of Christ greater riches than the treasures in Egypt; for he looked to the reward. By faith he forsook Egypt, not fearing the wrath of the king; for he persevered as seeing Him who is invisible" (Hebrews 11:24-27 NKJV).

Notice the action words of his difficult decisions: refused, chose, forsook, endured. He refused fame and fortune to choose identification with the oppressed people of God. He forsook Egypt to persevere in the wilderness because he had eternal perspective.

Moses could make difficult choices and sacrifices in this temporal world because he had his eyes on eternal reward. He said "no" to the passing pleasures of sin because he esteemed *"the reproach of Christ greater riches than the treasures in Egypt..."* (v.26).

Moses is a good example for Christians living in our highly materialistic world. His advice to us would be: *"Set your mind on things above, not on things on the earth"* (Colossians 3:2 NKJV).

Day Fifty-Three

The Name of the Lord

Ten of the compound Hebrew names for God from the Old Testament are listed below. Each reveals an aspect of His character. Looking up the verses listed would be a rewarding devotional exercise this week. You will discover that, in the meanings of His names, God has revealed Himself as a loving Father who is able to care for, protect and meet the needs of His children.

Jehovah-Rohi: The Lord my Shepherd (Psalm 23:1)

Jehovah-Shammah: The Lord Who is Present (Ezekiel 48:35)

Jehovah-Rapha: The Lord Our Healer (Exodus 16:26)

Jehovah-Tsidkenu: The Lord Our Righteousness (Jeremiah 23:6)

Jehovah-Jireh: The Lord Will Provide (Genesis 22:13-14)

Jehovah-Shalom: The Lord is Peace (Judges 6:24)

El-Elyon: The Most High God (Genesis 14:17-20)

El-Roi: The Strong One Who Sees (Genesis 16:12)

El-Shaddai: God Almighty (Genesis 17:1, Psalm 91:1)

El-Olam: The Everlasting God (Isaiah 40:28-31)

"He who dwells in the secret place of the Most High shall abide under the shadow of the Almighty (El-Shaddai). I will say of the Lord, 'He is my refuge and my fortress; My God, in Him will I trust.'" (Psalm 91:1-2 NKJV)

Day Fifty-Four

Principles of Prayer That Get Results

1. Pray with confidence. *"…the prayer of the upright is His delight!"* (Proverbs 15:8 NKJV). *"…we have confidence to enter the most Holy Place by the blood of Jesus"* (Hebrews 10:19 NIV).

2. Pray in faith. *"Therefore I say to you, whatever things you ask when you pray, believe that you receive them, and you will have them"* (Mark 11:24 NKJV).

3. Pray according to God's will. *"Now this is the confidence that we have in Him, that if we ask anything according to His will, He hears us. And if we know that He hears us, whatever we ask, we know that we have the petitions that we have asked of Him"* (1 John 5:14-15 NKJV).

4. Pray with a thankful heart. *"Don't worry about anything; instead, pray about everything; tell God your needs and don't forget to thank Him for His answers"* (Philippians 4:6 TLB).

Day Fifty-Five

Burning Hearts

"And they said to one another, Did not our heart burn within us while He talked with us on the road, and while He opened The Scriptures to us?" (Luke 24:32)

These are the words of the two discouraged disciples who encountered the resurrected Jesus on the road to Emmaus. They were sad because Jesus had been crucified and they didn't have faith to believe what He had spoken concerning the resurrection.

"Then He said to them, "O foolish ones, and slow of heart to believe in all that the prophets have spoken!" (v. 25).

But something happened that renewed their faith and rekindled their fire. Jesus opened the scriptures to them.

Do you need help to overcome sadness or discouragement? You can find strength in God's Word. Do you want to experience personal revival – even in trying times? The key is found in these words: "He opened the scriptures to them."

Jeremiah found joy and victory in trying times by feeding on the Word of God. So can you.

"Thy words were found and I did eat them; and Thy word was unto me the joy and rejoicing of my heart…" (Jeremiah 15:16 KJV).

Day Fifty-Six

Transforming Tragedy into Triumph

"The worst thing that happens to you can be the best thing that happens to you, depending on what you do with it."
~Oral Roberts

We have all been inspired by stories of people who overcame severe handicaps, rose above great obstacles and turned what could have been tragedy into triumph. Their attitude toward the adversity largely determined the outcome.

Our attitude toward God and His word during a time of difficulty will often determine whether we lose ground or gain ground spiritually. No one enjoys the hard times but we have to admit, "it is often the hard times that keeps our soul close to God." Persecution or difficulty can actually make you strong, if you let it. Drawing near to God during times of struggle or sorrow produces greater dependence on Him and leads to intimacy in our relationship. Even discouraging circumstances and disappointment can result in good if they cause us to draw near to God.

"Before I was afflicted I went astray, but now I keep your word…It is good for me that I have been afflicted, that I may learn your statutes" (Psalm 119:67 and 71 NKJV).

Are you facing a problem or passing through a struggle? Are you tempted to worry over the uncertainties of life?

Have difficulties and trying circumstances left you feeling discouraged? There will never be a better time to draw near to God than now.

"Be of good courage and He will strengthen your heart, all you who hope in the Lord" (Psalm 31:24 NKJV).

"This certain hope of being saved is a strong and trustworthy anchor for your souls, connecting us with God himself" (Hebrews 6:19 LB).

Day Fifty-Seven

Count Your Blessings

"When you are discouraged,
Don't sit down and frown;
Just get a piece of paper
And write your blessings down."

Discouragement can cause temporary loss of memory. In the midst of discouragement Christians often forget the past goodness of God: how He encouraged you at other times when you were disappointed and down; how He came through for you after a time of waiting; how He gave you strength to persevere.

Remembering God's past help and blessings won't change the circumstances which have contributed to your present discouragement, but it will strengthen your faith and help you to believe that God will come through for you again.

"Bless the Lord, O my soul, and forget not all His benefits" (Psalm 103:2 NKJV).

The children of Israel who perished in the wilderness became disappointed and frustrated because things didn't go as they had hoped. Discouragement followed disappointment. In their discouraged state, they yielded to unbelief and forgot God's mighty power and past deliverance.

"They soon forgot His works; they waited not for His counsel" (Psalm 106:13 KJV).

They lost their faith in His promises and *"believed not His word"* (Psalm 106:24 KJV).

Joshua and Caleb were of a different spirit. They faced the same discouraging circumstances, the same difficult delays, but without doubting God. They remembered His mighty power which brought them out of Egypt and miraculously sustained them in the wilderness. They knew that their God was greater than the obstacles, bigger than the giants, and therefore proclaimed, *"...we are well able to overcome it"* (Numbers 13:30 KJV).

I want to challenge you to stir up your faith today by remembering, as Joshua and Caleb did, and proclaiming by faith, "I am able to overcome it." Say to your problem, your discouragement, your disease: "I am able to overcome you."

Where did Joshua and Caleb get such faith? It came from a solid assurance that *"The Lord is with us"* (Numbers 14:9 KJV). God is with you. God will help you, just as He has in times past, if you will remember and believe.

Day Fifty-Eight

You Have To "Milk" Your Mind

Natives in nations like Thailand milk the poison from Cobras and sell it at a good price to be used as an antidote to snakebite. You wouldn't want the job. To "milk" The deadly poison the native must first get the cobra to strike. As the cobra strikes, he quickly grabs him behind the head and squeezes under its jaws to force its mouth open. Then he inserts his finger and presses the venom producing glands to force a few drops of the white poison into a vial. Three hours later the cobra will have a fresh supply of venom and be ready for milking again.

That's how it is with our minds. The poison of negative thoughts must be milked out regularly. But if the poison gets through the mind and into the spirit before it can be milked out, the antidote of God's word must be administered immediately.

That's why it is vital to pray at regular intervals and take in the word of God day after day.

"Evening, and morning, and at noon, will I pray, and cry aloud: and He shall hear my voice" (Psalm 55:17 KJV).

"My son, give attention to my words;...Do not let them depart from your eyes; Keep them in the midst of your heart; For they are life to those who find them, And health to all their flesh" (Proverbs 4:20-22 NKJV).

Negative thinking is like the venom of the serpent which, if not purged by prayer and the word, will inflame the mind and poison the spirit.

Here's the good news. If you have been bitten by the serpent of negative thinking or unbelief, the antidote is on hand. The word of God can neutralize the poison and get you back on the healthy ground of faith.

"Faith comes by hearing, and hearing by the word of God" (Romans 10:17 NKJV).

Day Fifty-Nine

You Are Smarter Than You Think You Are

"The fear of the Lord is the beginning of wisdom, and the knowledge of the Holy One is understanding" (Proverbs 9:10 NKJV).

If you fear (reverence) God you are wiser than the majority of people in the world today. In fact, if you reverence God, you are wiser than: the majority of college professors in the USA; the majority of politicians, presidents and world leaders; the majority of doctors, lawyers and corporate executives. How can this be? The majority of people in the preceding list don't know God, and therefore don't fear him. They don't have an ounce of the wisdom the Bible talks about. You didn't know you were so smart, did you?

You got the right kind of wisdom when you gave your life to Jesus and began to reverence God; you got the kind of wisdom that can get you from earth to heaven.

That's why I can say with certainty that you are wiser than the most intelligent, unsaved college professor in the world. He may have a head filled with worldly wisdom but he doesn't know what you know – how to make the journey from heaven to earth.

Now that I've convinced you that you are smarter than you thought I want to challenge you to be smart enough to use the wisdom God gave you! The wisdom of God will lead you. It will teach you to turn away from sin and draw near to God; it will teach you to pray, spend time in the word and attend church regularly; it will remind you how important it is to do the will of God.

The Bible says that wisdom is: *"better than the profits of silver, and her gain than fine gold. She is more precious than rubies, And all the things you may desire cannot compare with her"* (Proverbs 3 NKJV).

There is only one thing worse than being like the ungodly person who hasn't even come to the beginning of wisdom – being a Christian who doesn't use the God-given wisdom he possesses. If you are wise, you will do what wisdom tells you to do – love God with all your heart, serve Him faithfully, and seek His kingdom first.

Why not put wisdom to work right now by renewing your commitment to do the will of God?

"Wisdom is the principal thing...How much better it is to get wisdom than gold! And to get understanding is to be chosen rather than silver" (Proverbs 4:7; 16:16 NKJV).

Day Sixty

With All Your Heart

"The sacrifice of the wicked is an abomination to the LORD, But the prayer of the upright is His delight" (Proverbs 15:8 NKJV).

"The LORD is far from the wicked, But He hears the prayer of the righteous" (Proverbs 15:29 NKJV).

God delights in you. You are the joy of His heart. And He delights in your prayers.

If you want to make your Heavenly Father happy, express your love and gratitude in worship and release your faith in prayer.

Jeremiah gives us the key to answered prayer:

"Then you will call upon Me and go and pray to Me, and I will listen to you. And you will seek Me and find Me, when you search for Me with all your heart" (Jeremiah 29:12-13 NKJV).

Day Sixty-One

A Great Mystery

"For this cause shall a man leave his father and mother, and shall be joined unto his wife, and they two shall be one flesh. This is a great mystery: but I speak concerning Christ and the church" (Ephesians 5:31-32 NKJV).

The church is called the "Body of Christ" and also the "Bride of Christ". The great mystery referred to here is that just as Eve was taken out of Adam and then brought back to him as his wife, so the church came forth from Jesus and will be brought back to Him as His bride at the second coming. Just as husband and wife become one flesh, so we are one spirit with Christ, the Head of the body--the church (1 Corinthians 6:17; Ephesians 1:22-23).

Just as Adam carried Eve within himself before she was taken out of him, so Jesus carried the Church within Himself, even before He came into the world: *"According as He has chosen us in Him before the foundation of the world..."* (Ephesians 1:4 Darby). Bob Yandian says that "Jesus carried the spirit and soul of the Church inside Himself. Then, when He went to the cross, His side was opened up (just as Adam's side was opened when God formed Eve). At Pentecost, God began to build the Body of Christ from the "rib" of Jesus..."

In the same way that Eve was presented by God to Adam the day is coming when God will present the Bride of Christ to His Son, as a glorious church without spot or wrinkle (Ephesians 5:27).

Christians are naturally excited about the second coming and the reunion of the Heavenly Bridegroom with His earthly Bride--the Church. But did you ever stop to think that Jesus is excited, too? He is anxiously awaiting the glorious reunion with His Bride. Why? Yandian says it is because "He will be complete again--what was taken out of Him will be returned to Him."

Day Sixty-Two

You're In The Army Now

Christianity is not a "cake-walk" to heaven; it is a long, rigorous march through enemy territory. We are engaged in continual conflict with Satan and the powers of darkness (forces of evil) under his control. The world is not a Christian playground; it is a spiritual battle ground.

If you yield to the temptations of the enemy, you will be deceived. If you fail to resist him, you will be devoured. There are no alternatives to battle. You either fight or you are finished. The Christian who no longer struggles against evil is a Christian who has come under the power of darkness – the influence of evil.

We are in the last days. The time is short. God is putting together a lean, mean, spiritual fighting machine – and he wants you on the front lines!

You may (like Gideon in Judges 6 and 7) feel like a spiritual wimp, but God can make you a warrior. Interested? Here's some advice for would-be-warriors from three great soldiers of the faith.

Peter - *"Be sober, be vigilant; because your adversary the devil, as a roaring lion, walks about seeking whom he may devour: resist him, steadfast in the faith..."* (1 Peter 5:8-9 NKJV).

Paul - *"... endure hardship as a good soldier of Jesus Christ" (2 Timothy 2:3* NKJV). *"Fight the good fight of faith..."* (1 Timothy 6:12 KJV). *"Put on the whole armor of God, that you may be able to stand against the wiles of the devil"* (Ephesians 6:11 NKJV).

James - *"Submit yourselves therefore to God. Resist the devil and he will flee from you"* (James 4:7 KJV).

It's time to stop "running from" and start "running after" the devil. You're in the army now!

Day Sixty-Three

How To Get Rid of a Spirit of Heaviness

"...To give them beauty for ashes, the oil of joy for mourning, the garment of praise for the spirit of heaviness..." (Isaiah 61:3 NKJV).

Heaviness can come from problems, pressures, trials, difficulties. It can result from disappointment, discouragement, pain, rejection, negative circumstances, etc. We would call a spirit of heaviness, depression. The above verse is good news for all who have lost their joy in the Lord. A spirit of heaviness is like a garment you can take off and replace with another garment--the garment of praise.

But how can you put on a garment of praise when surrounded with problems, weighted down with worries, beset with financial difficulty? Here's the key. It will work by faith.

When you can't rejoice in your circumstances, rejoice in your God.

"Though the fig tree may not blossom, nor fruit be on the vines, though the labor of the olive may fail, and the fields yield no food; though the flock be cut off from the fold, and there be no herd in the stalls-- yet I will rejoice in the Lord, I will joy in the God of my salvation. The Lord God is my strength; He will make my feet like deer's feet, and He will make me walk on my high hills" (Habakkuk 3:17-19 NKJV).

Here's something else to rejoice about even in the hard times.

"I will greatly rejoice in the Lord, my soul shall be joyful in my God; for He has clothed me with the garments of salvation, He has covered me with the robe of righteousness..." (Isaiah 61:10 NKJV).

Day Sixty-Four

The Positive Atmosphere of Praise

The Bible doesn't say "God inhabits the gripes, complaints and criticisms of His people." (That's where the devil lives)!   The Bible says God *"inhabits the praises"* of His people (Psalm 22:3 MEV). God feels welcome and wanted wherever He finds people who praise Him.

He lives in the positive atmosphere of praise. You don't have to wait until Sunday mornings for a visit. You can enjoy God's presence all week long, if you will be a praiser, not a complainer.

I can think of at least six times when you should praise God: when you feel like it, and when you don't; when you want to, and when you don't; when things are going well, and when they're not.

Praise is faith in action. Griping, complaining – negative thoughts and words – grieve the Holy Spirit; positive, faith-filled thoughts and words, expressed in praise, make Him happy.

Our praise goes before us to prepare the way into the presence of God.

"Enter into his gates with thanksgiving, and into his courts with praise: be thankful unto him, and bless his name" (Psalm 100:4 KJV).

Day Sixty-Five

It is Well

The Shunammite woman in 2 Kings 4 places her dead son on the bed, and immediately went looking for Elisha the prophet. She didn't waste time or words on people who could extend sympathy. She determined to find a man of God who had faith to fight the devil.

When Elisha's servant, Gehazi, asked "how are you doing" she responded, "*It is well*" and kept on going. (2 Kings 4:26 KJV)

What an amazing response! These are the words of a determined woman with a violent faith—a faith that will fight the devil to take back a stolen blessing. Her "I won't take no for an answer" faith compelled the prophet to go with her, and resulted in a miraculous resurrection. With a violent faith she took hold of God and didn't let go until the battle was won.

The Shunammite woman had something many of us have lost—"fight". When you stop believing and start whining, you have lost your fight; when you stop praising and start complaining, you have lost your fight; when you stop claiming victory and start confessing defeat, you have lost your fight.

Has the devil left you laying by the side of the road wounded, discouraged and defeated? Have you become weak and passive, too weary to go on?

Well, God hasn't forsaken you. He has a word for you.

"Don't give up. Get up!"

If you give up, you will lay there in your apathy until the devil drains every drop of faith and victory out of you. Stop feeling sorry for yourself and get up. You don't need pity, you need power—power to fight and take back what the devil took from you. Don't sit down and quit. Get up and fight.

"Fight the good fight of faith, lay hold on eternal life" (1 Timothy 6:12 KJV).

Day Sixty-Six

Why God Chose Mary for a Special Task

"And she will bring forth a Son, and you shall call His name JESUS, for He will save His people from their sins. So all this was done that it might be fulfilled which was spoken by the Lord through the prophet, saying: 'Behold, the virgin shall be with child, and bear a Son, and they shall call His name Immanuel,' which is translated, 'God with us'" (Matthew 1:21-23 NKJV).

Did you ever wonder why Mary was chosen above all the maidens in Israel for this great honor? The angel in Luke 1:30 (NKJV) said Mary had found favor with God. Several hints as to why she found favor and was chosen to be the earthly mother of Jesus are given in other verses of the first chapter of Luke.

1. She was a woman of Purity – v. 34

Mary was a young woman who was committed to live a holy life to the glory of God.

2. She was a woman of Faith – v. 38

Mary believed the angel's message and responded, *"Let it be to me according to your word"* (v. 45).

3. She was a woman of great Devotion – vs. 46-56

God loves people who worship Him in spirit and truth. Jesus said in John 4:23 that the Father seeks such people. It is evident from Mary's spontaneous song in vs. 46-56 that she was a worshipper; such beautiful, spontaneous expressions of praise do not flow from the heart of one who is not in the habit of daily worshipping the Lord.

4. She was a woman of Humility – v. 48

Mary's response was one of humility. She didn't have a proud attitude which sought recognition by drawing attention to herself. She wanted God to be glorified in her life. She was honored and humbled that God had chosen her. God loves this attitude. *"For thus says the High and Lofty One who inhabits eternity, whose name is Holy: 'I dwell in the high and holy place, with him who has a contrite and humble spirit…'"* (Isaiah 57:15 NKJV).

When one understands what a humble woman Mary was it is not difficult to imagine how grieved she is that people would exalt her, worship her and pray to her. She always wanted the glory – all the glory – to go to Jesus.

5. She was a woman of the Word – vs. 46-56

A good portion of Mary's song is scripture from the Old Testament which she had memorized. Perhaps this explains her purity. She could say with the Psalmist, *"Thy word have I hidden in my heart, that I might not sin against you"* (Psalm 119:11 KJV).

Day Sixty-Seven

How To "Demon-Proof" Your Life

"When an unclean spirit goes out of a man, he goes through dry places, seeking rest, and finds none. Then he says, 'I will return to my house from which I came.' And when he comes, he finds it empty, swept, and put in order. Then he goes and takes with him seven other spirits more wicked than himself, and they enter and dwell there; and the last state of that man is worse than the first. So shall it also be with this wicked generation" (Matthew 12:43-45 NKJV).

Demons look for empty houses (people) in which to live. They are fallen, disembodied spirits; to operate on earth they must possess and control – or oppress and influence – human beings.

So, how can you "demon-proof" your life? By being filled with the Spirit and the Word. There's no room for a demon in a spirit-filled house. If the fullness of the mighty Spirit of God dwells in you, demons won't even be comfortable dropping in for a visit. (They might "drop by" but they won't "drop in").

"You (that means you!) *Are of God...and have overcome them (evil spirits): because greater is He who is in you, than he who is in the world"* (1 John 4:4 NKJV). If you are filled with the Spirit, and filled up on God's word, demons won't find any open doors or empty spaces at your house.

"...you are strong, and the word of God abides (lives) *in you, and you have overcome the wicked one"* (1 John 2:14 NKJV)."

Day Sixty-Eight

The Promised Gift

"...what shall we do? Peter answered, 'Repent and be baptized every one of you in the name of Jesus Christ for the remission of sins, and ye shall receive the gift of the Holy Ghost. For the promise is unto you, and to your children, and to all that are afar off, even as many as the Lord our God shall call" (Acts 2:37-39 KJV).

"I am confident that we have no conception of the change that would come if, with one heart and one soul, we were to take our place with the first disciples at the footstool of our ascended Lord, and with one accord claim the promised gift." (Andrew Murray)

The fullness of God's spirit is the privilege of every believer who prepares his heart and claims the promise. *"...How much more shall your Heavenly Father give the Holy Spirit to them that ask Him"* (Luke 11:13 KJV)?

The keys to receiving the fullness of the Holy Spirit are desire and faith.

"Blessed are those which do hunger and thirst after righteousness: for they shall be filled" (Matthew 5:6 KJV).

"...whatever things you ask when you pray, believe that you receive them, and you will have them" (Mark 11:24 NKJV).

Day Sixty-Nine

God Wants You to Win

"Therefore we also, since we are surrounded by so great a cloud of witnesses, let us lay aside every weight, and the sin which so easily ensnares us, and let us run with endurance the race that is set before us" (Hebrews 12:1 NKJV).

It's hard to run when you are weighted down or bound up. God wants to set you free to run the Christian race with joy and victory. He wants you to finish. He wants you to win.

That's why He wants to break the chains that bind you and lift your heavy load. God is here to help you today. Reach out and take hold of victory by faith. Open up and receive the supernatural power of God.

"…and the yoke shall be destroyed because of the anointing" (Isaiah 10:27 KJV).

Day Seventy

God Will Bring You Through

(Part of this message was excerpted from a letter by David Wilkerson.)

"Satan has come against many with fury and force to bring you down and destroy your faith. Your despair, fear and troubles are not a result of sin. Your way out of this struggle is to humble yourself before the Lord. Go to prayer regularly and spread it all out before Him. Trust in God to bring you through. He is going to deliver you. (Psalm 91:15).

You feel like a spiritual cripple – useless, boxed in – and you see no joy or usefulness ahead. You have a feeling of emptiness as though you are accomplishing nothing…Even prayer seems useless – your spirit is dry, and you are just surviving.

Take hope! God has not hidden His eyes from you. He is going to bring His sunshine back into your soul. But you must step out in childlike faith and trust (Psalm 37:3-4).

You are mourning because of someone or something you lost. You have a spirit of grief and sadness that will not go away…I have a word for you, right from God's throne: You can laugh again! God wants to supernaturally bring you out of your depression.

But the only power to set you free is in His Word! Get back to the Word!

"Thy words were found and I did eat them; and Thy Word was unto me the joy and the rejoicing of mine heart" (Jeremiah 15:16 KJV).

Day Seventy-One

Faith To Succeed, Faith To Survive

Before Joseph could succeed by faith he had to survive by faith. The devil knows that the vision Joseph had as a teenager was of God. He also knew that to stop its fulfillment he had to somehow steal Joseph's faith.

Joseph's life is a great example of someone who held on to God by faith through trial after trial. His brothers plotted to kill him, threw him into a pit and then sold him into slavery. Joseph served his master faithfully, but when he refused the advances of Potiphar's lust-driven wife, she falsely accused him and he was thrown into prison.

Joseph had lots of opportunities for self pity and bitterness while languishing in prison. But by faith he forgave, and by faith he took hold of the favor of God. Joseph's faith in the face of adversity helped him become powerful, not pitiful – better, not bitter.

The same faith that enabled him to survive in prison helped him succeed in the palace. *"But the Lord was with Joseph, and showed him mercy, and gave him favor in the sight of the keeper of the prison"* (Genesis 39:21 NKJV).

"He sent a man before them, even Joseph who was sold for a servant: whose feet they hurt with fetters: he was laid in iron (they put an iron collar on his neck!): *Until the time that his word came: the word of the Lord tried him. The king sent and loosed him;…He made him lord of his house* (the palace!) *and ruler of all his substance"* (Psalm 105:17-21 KJV).

Day Seventy-Two

Open The Gates!

"That in blessing I will bless thee, and in multiplying I will multiply thy seed as the stars of the heaven, and as the sand which is upon the sea shore: and thy seed shall posses the gate of his enemies" (Genesis 22:17 KJV).

A gate is the entrance into a house, a city, a fortress, etc. It is also used in scripture to signify power or dominion (Cruden's Unabridged Concordance).

The idea here is that the seed of Abraham would multiply in the earth, grow stronger and conquer their enemies. The promise includes believers of all generations:

"And if you are Christ's, then you are Abraham's seed, and heirs according to the promise" (Galatians 3:26 NKJV).

Jesus said in Matthew 16:18 (KJV), *"...upon this Rock I will build my church; and the gates of hell shall not prevail against it."*

This verse points to the ultimate triumph of the Kingdom of God over the kingdom of darkness by the authority Jesus has imparted to the church. It also has specific application for us today. Hell has built gates all around us. Some are meant to hinder spiritual progress or to prevent access to heaven's storehouse; others are used to hold back blessings directed toward us, or to hoard blessings stolen from us.

They are invisible gates, guarded by spiritual enemies. In order to tear them down, we must first overcome the demonic powers guarding them (Ephesians 6:12). We must rise up with a violent faith to take what our spiritual enemies have held back, and to take back what they have stolen. Armed with the promises of Genesis 22:17 and Matthew 16:18, we are destined to win: if we rise up and fight.

"From the time of John the Baptizer until now, the kingdom of heaven has been forcefully advancing, and forceful people have been seizing it. (the violent take it by force)" (Matthew 11:12 (NOG and KJV).

Day Seventy-Three

"Jesus, It's For You!"

We have suggested that, when the devil knocks on your door and attempts to deliver a package you don't care to receive, you should let Jesus answer. Our suggestion is rooted in scripture!

David knew how to get strength from God to stand against his enemies: *"it is God who arms me with strength…"* (Psalm 18:32 NKJV). He also knew how to cry out to God for help when his enemies seemed too strong for him:

"In my distress I called upon the Lord, And cried out to my God; He heard my voice from His temple, And my cry came before Him, even to His ears…He delivered me from my strong enemy, and from them which hated me: for they were too strong for me" (Psalm 18:6, 17 NKJV).

David learned that God would come to his aid, that He would stand up to defend him: *"Plead my cause, O Lord, with them that strive with me: fight against them that fight against me. Take hold of shield and buckler, and stand up for mine help"* (Psalm 35:1-2 KJV).

"Put on your armor, take your shield and protect me by standing in front" (Psalm 35:2 LB).

You can be bold when the devil comes to your house, if you are convinced that Jesus will stand between him and you!

Paul knew that Jesus stood ready to help and defend him, too. He wrote 2 Timothy from prison in Rome shortly before his martyrdom. He reflects on a particularly difficult struggle in chapter 4 and then ends with these words of confidence:

"At my first defense no one stood with me…But the Lord stood with me and strengthened me… I was delivered out of the mouth of the lion. And the Lord will deliver me from every evil work and preserve me for His heavenly kingdom" (2 Timothy 4:16-18 NKJV).

Day Seventy-Four

The Blood Covering

Under the old covenant, sins were not removed; they were just atoned for, or covered. Through the blood of the New Covenant, the sinless blood of Christ, sin is not only covered, it is removed. We have been delivered from the penalty and the power of sin.

"...our old man (nature) was crucified with Him, that the body of sin might be done away with, that we should no longer be slaves of sin" (Romans 6:6 NKJV).

"For sin shall not have dominion over you, for you are not under the law but under grace" (Romans 6:14 NKJV).

But there is still a blood covering. To live under the covering of the blood of Jesus is to live under God's protection. It is symbolized by the Passover in Egypt when the death angel passed over houses where the blood of the sacrifice lamb had been applied (Exodus 12). By active faith in the power of the shed blood of Jesus Christ, we claim the blessings bought for us by Christ on the cross: one of which is spiritual covering and protection.

We also claim righteousness by faith based on the covering of the blood of Jesus.

"For He made Him, who knew no sin to be sin for us, that we might become the righteousness of God in Him" (2 Corinthians 5:21 NKJV).

I think my favorite verse on covering is Isaiah 61:10 (NKJV): *"I will greatly rejoice in the Lord, my soul shall be joyful in my*

God; For He has clothed me with the garments of salvation. He has covered me with the robe of righteousness…"

The robes of righteousness we wear all come from the same fabric: the blood stained garments of the precious Lamb of God who takes away the sin of the world!

Day Seventy-Five

Precious Promises

"Grace and peace be multiplied to you in the knowledge of God and of Jesus our Lord, as His divine power has given to us all things that pertain to life and godliness, through the knowledge of Him who called us by glory and virtue, by which have been given to us exceedingly great and precious promises, that through these you may be partakers of the divine nature, having escaped the corruption that is in the world through lust" (1 Peter 1:2-5 NKJV).

Three words in these verses – power, promises, partakers – point to our potential in Christ. Great resources have already been made available to us: "his divine power has given to us all things that pertain to life and godliness." These things come to us through "the knowledge of Him." The power is harnessed and then released when we learn the promises of God and act upon them in faith: When we feed on His promises, we partake of His nature.

Potentially the power is here. It exists within you, around you. The power to live a godly life, to change, to overcome is here, just waiting for believing Christians to tap into it by faith.

Electricity potentially was here from the beginning of time. The power existed all around the human race. But for many years human beings didn't know how to harness or use it. Great reservoirs of power were always stored in mountain lakes, but only in modern times have we learned how to convert that potential power into energy and light.

There is untapped potential around you, in you. You can tap into it by studying God's word and thereby growing in the knowledge of Jesus, by acting on the promises in faith and thereby partaking of the divine nature.

Day Seventy-Six

The Power and Beauty of a Holy Life

In the third chapter of his first epistle, Peter gives instructions to men and women on godly living, attitudes, and relationships. He encourages us to live in harmony with one another, to be kind, considerate, compassionate, and humble (v. 8). He instructs husbands to treat their wives with honor and respect, and he instructs Christian wives to live holy lives in submission to their husbands (v. 1-2, 7). Godly attitudes manifested in holy living are pleasing in the sight of God.

"Your beauty should not come from outward adornment, such as elaborate hairstyles and the wearing of gold jewelry or fine clothes. ⁴ Rather, it should be that of your inner self, the unfading beauty of a gentle and quiet spirit, which is of great worth in God's sight." (1 Peter 3:3-5 NIV). God looks on the heart, and He rejoices when He finds the beauty of a submissive and gentle spirit in a godly woman.

The term "beauty of a quiet spirit" is not intended to imply quietness in the sense of shyness or not talking. It has to do with self control, quiet assurance and trust in God. Sarah is given as an example of a woman with such inner beauty, not only because of her purity and submission, but because of her confidence and faith in God.

"By faith Sarah herself received ability to conceive, even beyond the proper time of life, since she considered Him

faithful who had promised" (Hebrews 11:11 NASB).

This is the picture of a godly woman God paints – a woman who reflects the inner beauty of a quiet and gentle spirit in submission, holy living, and faith. Such beauty is precious – "of great worth" – in God's sight. Such women are worthy of honor and respect.

Day Seventy-Seven

The Need for Spiritual Discernment

We need spiritual discernment today as never before. We need to diligently apply and obey the Word of God. We need to place greater emphasis on character and hold preachers to higher standards of conduct. The Bible is filled with warnings such as the one in 1 John 4:1(KJV):

"Believe not every spirit, but try the spirits whether they are of God: because many false prophets are gone out into the world."

"John points out that many spirits (that is, prophets who speak of spiritual things) have gone out into the world. It is therefore necessary that the Christian make a practice of testing preachers to see whether they come from God or not. One test to be applied is given in 1 John 4:2-3, 'The true preacher…centers his message in Christ' (not in the blessings Christ brings, not in spiritual experiences, not in signs and wonders done in Christ's name)." (The Biblical Expositor, A.J. Holman. Philadelphia, 1960).

We should seek and be open to supernatural manifestations of God's spirit, but we should not be overly impressed by them. Church history is filled with accounts of men who performed miracles under a strong supernatural anointing, and yet they were not true servants of God. This shocks Christians who are focused more on the manifestations than on the message, more on the charisma of the messenger than on his character.

But we should not be surprised that miracles are sometimes performed by men who are not true servants of Christ. Jesus said, *"Many will say to Me in that day, 'Lord, Lord have we not prophesied in Thy name? And in Thy name have we not cast out devils? And in Thy name done many wonderful works?' And then will I profess unto them, 'I never knew you: depart from me, ye that work iniquity'"* (Matthew 7:22-23 KJV).

"And Jesus answered and said unto them, Take heed that no man deceive you...And many false prophets shall rise, and shall deceive many...For there shall arise false Christs, and false prophets, and shall shew great signs and wonders; insomuch that, if it were possible, they shall deceive the very elect" (Matthew 24:4, 11, 24 KJV).

God desires that we hunger for the supernatural, but we should not exalt supernatural experience to the extent that we fail to clearly discern a man's character, or his spirit.

"Beware of false prophets, which come to you in sheep's clothing, but inwardly they are ravening wolves. Ye shall know them by their fruits..." (Matthew 7:15-16 KJV).

The "fruits" here are not signs and wonders performed under a supernatural anointing. They are the products of a godly life, of doing the will of God, of walking in obedience to the Word of God (Matthew 7:20-24).

One of the keys to spiritual discernment is remembering that "We must judge our experience by the Word. We must never judge the word by our experience."

Day Seventy-Eight

Discerning Between Good and Evil

"Then you shall again discern between the righteous and the wicked, between one who serves God and one who does not serve Him" (Malachi 3:18 NKJV).

"But solid food belongs to those who are full of age, that is, those why by reason of use have their senses exercised to discern both good and evil" (Hebrews 5:14 NKJV).

Discernment is a faculty of both mind and spirit. Discerning between good and evil involves both mental and spiritual judgment and perception. A renewed mind, submitted to the Spirit of God and nourished by the Word of God, is not something to be shut down or turned off when the need for spiritual discernment arises. The Bible tells us to *"Lean not on your own understanding"* (Proverbs 3:5 NKJV), but this does not mean that we should turn off our minds. We should submit them to the Spirit and to the Word and then exercise them in discerning between good and evil.

A question or doubt raised by a renewed mind should not be ignored, discarded or rationalized away. We are spirit beings, but we should not divorce mind and spirit. There is an "inter-connectedness" created by God between spirit and soul (mind, will and emotions).

In the early days of the Jesus movement, we cautioned people not to turn off or empty their minds because of the dangers of succumbing to demonic influence when in a passive or trance-like mental state. We understood the danger because this had happened to many who got involved in Eastern mysticism, transcendental meditation, etc.

Jessie Penn-Lewis, in her classic work War on the Saints, also warned of the dangers of letting someone talk you into turning off your mind.

"Satan works to arouse and excite the natural life, under the guise of its being spiritual. The false conception of 'surrender' as yielding the body to supernatural power, with the mind ceasing to act, is the highest subtlety of the enemy…WE have also pointed out again and again that 'claiming the blood' cannot protect us from the enemy if in any way he is given ground, e.g., if the cerebral nerves cease to act by 'letting the mind go bland,' and the vegetative nerves are awakened to act in their place, so that the latter are excited to give 'thrills' and 'streams of life' through the body (cerebral nerves – of the cerebral system; the central region of the nervous system. Vegetative nerves – the lower nerve centers of the ganglionic system. (Dr. Naum Katik, p. 145-6 quoted in the Overcomer 1920).

Moreover, the arousing of the 'vegetative nerves' to such abnormal activity that 'floods of life' have appeared to pour through the whole body – the enemy whispering at the same moment, 'this is Divine –'

(1) dulls the mind and makes it inert in action
(2) causes a craving in the recipient for more of the 'Divine' life
(3) leads to the danger of the ministration of it to others…"

(War on the Saints by Jessie Penn-Lewis, p. 144-9. Overcomer Literary Trust, Dorest England. Printed in the U.S.A. by Christian Literature Crusade, Fort Washington, PA).

I join Jessie Penn-Lewis, and a host of other Christian writers who through the centuries have warned against 'letting the mind go blank.' Don't turn your mind off. Make it be an ally of your spirit in discerning between good and evil. Further, if you find yourself in a meeting where a preacher encourages you to turn your mind off, or let your mind go, I urge you to let yourself go out the nearest exit! If you do stay, resist the spirit of that preacher and the message he brings.

There is truth in the old proverb, "an idle mind is the devil's workshop." A turned off or bland mind is fertile soil for supernatural activity of the demonic kind.

God gave you your mind. If you are following Jesus, He is renewing it. Don't shut it down. Sharpen it, exercise it, and use it for His glory.

Day Seventy-Nine

Faith with a Foundation

"By faith Sarah herself also received strength to conceive seed, and she bore a child when she was past the age, because she judged Him faithful who had promised" (Hebrews 11:11 NKJV).

Faith is only as valid as the object in which it is placed. The faith of the Christian is grounded in eternal truth – and in the One who spoke the truth. It is faith with a foundation; faith based on fact.

This is intelligent faith. It goes beyond reason, but it is not unreasonable. This is faith with wisdom. It is not foolish. This is not faith which operates by formulas. It is faith which operates in obedience to the Word of God.

Credible Bible faith believes and obeys the Word of God. It is more focused on obeying than obtaining. It is after God Himself, not just what He gives; obtaining blessings is a by-product of obedience.

This faith is out to please God, not self. It is more concerned with holiness than happiness; happiness is a by-product of holiness.

"By faith Abel offered to God a more excellent sacrifice" (Hebrews 11:4 KJV).

"By faith Enoch was translated…for he had this testimony, that he pleased God" (Hebrews 11:5 KJV).

"By faith Noah…became heir of the righteousness which is by faith" (Hebrews 11:7 KJV).

"By faith Abraham…obeyed" (Hebrews 11:8 KJV).

Day Eighty

Conditioned for Containment

"Why do we sit here until we die?" (2 Kings 7:1-20 NLV).

Satan wants to contain you. Why? To keep you from advancing; to prevent you from doing damage to his kingdom.

Containment is a military strategy. The word "contain" has the idea of "being held within bounds." Another definition is "to hold back or within fixed limits." Satan wants to determine your boundaries, but the Christian should permit no one but God to draw the lines around his or her life. Through deception, Satan has conditioned us for containment. We become accustomed to it; we accept it; we adapt to it. God wants to help us break out.

To break out we must change our thinking. Satan is a deceiver. He tries to pass himself off as an all-powerful foe. The truth is, he is a snake with a crushed head. Jesus destroyed him and devastated his kingdom.

So why does he yield such power today? People let him. Satan's only power is what he usurps from people through deception. Jesus said, *"All power* (authority) *is given unto Me…"* (Matthew 28:18 KJV). God didn't leave any for the devil. Valid authority is held by Jesus and those to whom He delegates it.

The second thing we need to change is our speaking. We need to say what the Bible says about Satan and the powers of darkness. The Bible says they are defeated foes, destroyed by the Lord Jesus (Hebrews 2:14-15). The Bible says they are under the authority of the Lord Jesus (Philippians 2:9-11). The Bible says that believers have authority over them (Mark 16:18; Ephesians 1:18-23). The Bible says that we can overcome them by the Word (1 John 2:14). The Bible says they will flee from believers who submit to God and resist the devil (James 4:7).

Finally, to break out of containment you must change your behavior. If you have been a passive prisoner, it's time to pick up the sword of the Spirit (the word of God) and go after the devil. If you have been an apathetic worshipper, it's time to put your heart into it. Do something surprising, something the devil is not expecting. Do what the Bible says: clap, shout, lift up your hands, lift up your voice, and begin to praise God with all your heart.

You're on your way! The devil can't contain a believer who has a sword in his hand and a song in his mouth (Psalm 149:6-9).

Remember the lepers in 2 Kings 7 who said, "Why sit here until we die?" Well, they didn't sit there. They got up and did something – something unexpected. They broke out. They ran toward the camp of the enemy! And God made their foot beats sound like a mighty army – so mighty that the enemy army fled and left all their goods behind.

Day Eighty-One

A Future and a Hope

"For I know the plans that I have for you, declares the Lord, plans for welfare and not for calamity to give you a future and a hope" (Jeremiah 29:11 NASB).

God has plans for you and they are good. We challenge you to seek God with your whole heart and pursue His purpose for your life.

God's plans are better than your plans. God's ways are better than your ways. God's will is better than your will. If you get what you want while ignoring what God wills it will not satisfy you. The world is filled with people who achieved their goals, saw their plans fulfilled, and yet they are unhappy. Why? True happiness comes from discovering and doing the will of God. True fulfillment comes from pursuing God's plans for your life, not your plans for your life.

"…Don't let the world around you squeeze you into its own mold, but let God remold your minds from within, so you may prove in practice that the plan of God for you is good…" (Romans 12:2 Phillips).

Day Eighty-Two

The Glory Before You

"By faith Abraham obeyed when he was called to go out to the place which he would receive as an inheritance. And he went out, not knowing where he was going. By faith he dwelt in the land of promise as in a foreign country, dwelling in tents with Isaac and Jacob, the heirs with him of the same promise; for he waited for the city which has foundations, whose builder and maker is God" (Hebrews 11:8-10 NKJV).

Abraham lived by faith. He kept looking up. That's what I want to encourage you to do. Sometimes trials and trouble blur our vision of heavenly things. Sometimes we lose sight of God's purpose in the midst of the everyday pressures and problems of life.

That's why it is so important to remember where you're headed – to remember your destiny and your destination. That's why we need to keep looking up and keep pressing on toward the "city which has foundations." Don't let the temporary darkness of this world dim your vision of the eternal glory before you.

You have a wonderful future – eternal joy in the presence of God. As you journey, keep looking up. And always remember, faithfulness in this life will be rewarded in the life to come.

"His lord said to him, 'Well done, good and faithful servant; you were faithful over a few things, I will make you ruler over many things. Enter into the joy of your Lord'" (Matthew 25:21 NKJV).

Day Eighty-Three

Content in Christ

"Not that I speak in regard to need, for I have learned in whatever state I am, to be content: I know how to be abased, and I know how to abound. Everywhere and in all things I have learned both to be full and to be hungry, both to abound and to suffer need. I can do all things through Christ who strengthens me" (Philippians 4:11-13 NKJV).

Paul's contentment in life was not dependent on positive circumstances. He sang praises at midnight when in prison. His contentment was not dependent on material prosperity. He experienced both abundance and lack at different times. I'm sure he preferred prosperity and abundance, but he was content during times of deprivation and need.

What was Paul's secret? His contentment was not tied to possessions but to a person. In times of plenty and in times of lack, his source of joy was the same – Jesus. Paul's secret was an intimate, fulfilling relationship with Jesus.

Paul walked in the spirit. Faith in Jesus connected him to the spiritual realm. He was "in" this world, but not "of" it. He lived with an attitude of "Divine Detachment." He didn't have a poverty spirit. Paul knew how to enjoy the "good life." But the loss of material possessions didn't do him in – why? He enjoyed them but he was not overly dependent on or attached to them. He was attached to Jesus.

Paul had a loose grip on the world and a firm grip on Jesus. That's why he could say, *"I have learned the secret of being content in any and every situation…"* (Philippians 4:12 NIV).

Day Eighty-Four

Victors, Not Victims

Jesus resisted and overcame the devil by the spoken word (Matthew 4). James tells us that if we will resist the devil he will flee (James 4). Our resisting must include bold verbal assaults with the word of God – the sword of the Spirit (Ephesians 6:17).

We must confront the powers of darkness with a faith-filled testimony of truth – the truth of God's word. We must plead the blood of Jesus and declare that they have no right to trespass on God's property, that through Christ's death they have been destroyed (Hebrews 2:14), and that the cross has cancelled all their claims against us (Colossians 2:14-15).

We are victors in Christ (Romans 8:37). We shouldn't be talking or acting like victims. We must enforce the victory by faith with the authority Jesus has given us. We must not allow the powers of darkness to intimidate us. We must declare that they are defeated, that their power is broken. We must address them directly and command them to go in Jesus' name (Mark 16:17).

Satan's attacks often come in the form of demonic assaults against the mind or in the soul. When we sense demonic influence on our thoughts or emotions we must not yield to it; instead, we should immediately resist it. We must specifically resist fear, depression, lust, unbelief, etc. We must treat them as enemy soldiers, members of an evil invading army; we must resist immediately and ferociously; we must speak the word of God and order them to go in Jesus' name. Always remember Revelation 12:11 (KJV). Keep it in your spiritual arsenal. Be ready to use it at every moment. There is power and authority in the spoken word.

"They overcame him by the blood of the Lamb, and by the Word of their testimony."

Day Eighty-Five

The Power of Thoughts

Thoughts are the beginning of reality. You generally think about something before you say it (it's always best to use your head before you use your mouth). You generally think about something before you do it. And you generally think about something before you pray about it.

Since thoughts are the beginning of reality it's important to think the right thoughts. The best way to do that is to tune into God's frequency and pick up His thoughts. The Holy Spirit is broadcasting 24 hours a day.

"How precious are Thy thoughts unto me, O God! How great is the sum of them" (Psalm 139:17 KJV).

Since thoughts are the beginning of reality, we want to identify and reject evil, erroneous, or negative thoughts.

"Search me, O God, and know my heart: try me, and know my thoughts: And see if there be any wicked way in me, and lead me in the way everlasting" (Psalm 139:23-24 KJV).

The power of thoughts is released in words and actions. That's why we should pray with David: *"Set a watch, O Lord, before my mouth; keep the door of my lips. Incline not my heart to any evil thing, to practice wicked works…"* (Psalm 141:3-24 KJV).

Your life is shaped and controlled by images, impressions, and thoughts you place in your spirit. Your outlook will be good or evil, your attitude will be positive or negative, based on what you put in your spirit.

Thoughts are the beginning of reality; thoughts shape your destiny. The reality you want to experience, the destiny you want to go after, is the one that flows out of the mind of God. Pick up His thoughts, put them in your spirit, and you will experience the fulfillment that comes from walking in the ways of God.

"For I know the thoughts that I think toward you, saith the Lord, thoughts of peace, and not of evil, to give you an expected end (a future and a hope)" (Jeremiah 29:11 KJV/NKJV).

Isn't it good to know that God has you – and your future – on His mind? You're special. God is thinking about you.

Day Eighty-Six

The Garment of Praise

"Whoever offers praise glorifies Me; and to him who orders his conduct aright I will show the salvation of God" (Psalm 50:23 NKJV).

God is glorified when we praise Him – especially when we praise Him by faith during times when we don't feel like praising Him. Praise is faith at work.

Anybody can offer praise after deliverance is manifest, after the answer comes, when the blessing arrives. The challenge is always to praise Him before the trial is over, before the problem is solved, before the circumstances change.

We should praise God all the time – in good times and in hard times.

"Therefore by Him let us continually offer the sacrifice of praise to God, that is, the fruit of our lips, giving thanks to His name" (Hebrews 13:15 NKJV).

Praise is exalting God for what He does, and worship is exalting Him for who he is. When you don't feel like praising God for what He has done, you can praise Him for who He is. He is worthy of our praise.

Praise is a key to a life of victory. Praise may not immediately change the circumstances, but it will change you! Praise can influence your emotions. By an act of your will, you can release praise in faith and God's power will lift you out of depression and despair.

"...to console those who mourn in Zion, to give them beauty for ashes, the oil of joy for mourning, the garment of praise for the spirit of heaviness; that they may be called trees of righteousness, the planting of the Lord, that He may be glorified" (Isaiah 61:3 NKJV).

Day Eighty-Seven

The Ministry of Peace

"Peace I leave with you, My peace I give to you; not as the world gives do I give to you. Let not your heart be troubled, neither let it be afraid" (John 14:27 NKJV).

In the midst of the struggles and storms of life, peace ministers to the heart of the believer. Even in this troubled world, we can have peace because our peace comes from another world. We have peace because the Holy Spirit has taken up residence in our hearts (John 14:26).

Peace ministers to us and says *"Let not your heart be troubled, nor let it be fearful."* This verse indicates that we have a choice. We can choose not to be troubled when surrounded by troubles; we can choose not to be fearful when confronted by fear. Peace speaks the same language as faith – the language of the victorious Giver of peace, the language of heaven. It says, "don't let trouble and fear steal your confidence in God." It says, "pray, don't panic."

"Be anxious for nothing, but in everything by prayer and supplication, with thanksgiving, let your requests be made known to God; and the peace of God, which surpasses all understanding, will guard your hearts and minds through Christ Jesus" (Philippians 4:6-7 NKJV).

Day Eighty-Eight

Miracles in the Wilderness

"And you shall remember that the Lord your God led you all the way these forty years in the wilderness, to humble you and test you, to know what was in your heart, whether you would keep His commandments or not" (Deuteronomy 8:2 NKJV).

"We should understand the importance of the wilderness experiences in our lives. Many of us fear the wilderness times, those periods when it seems there's no growth or vision. We would much rather be in the middle of a dynamic worship service than a place of spiritual barrenness.

"But we should look at our wilderness experiences as preparation for greater growth. After we have been emptied of our good ideas, we're in a prime position to receive a fresh revelation from God.

"The wilderness is the perfect place for that revelation. It may be a trial or persecution, a season of spiritual inactivity where doubts assail us or a period of broken hopes and dreams…All wilderness experiences share certain characteristics: we are empty, inactive and at the end of our own resources…" (Tim Storey in Charisma Magazine, July 1994).

People find God when they get to the end of their own resources. People find God after long delays when hope is nearly gone. Miracles happen in the wilderness.
"They wandered in the wilderness in a desolate way; they found no city to dwell in. Hungry and thirsty, their soul fainted in them. Then they cried out to the Lord in their trouble, and He delivered them out of their distresses" (Psalm 107:4-6 NKJV).

Day Eighty-Nine

The Expectation of Hope

"And now abide faith, hope, love, these three; but the greatest of these is love" (1 Corinthians 13:13 NKJV).

Why is love the greatest of these three? Because it is the root, the source; faith and hope grow out of it.

Hope is one of the deepest needs of our society today. Multitudes are experiencing despair – the opposite of hope. The Christian has a basis for hope even in the face of despair because he/she has the assurance of God's unchanging love.

Hope is rooted in love. Simply defined hope is, "a feeling that what is wanted will happen; desire accompanied by expectation."

God's word encourages us to keep hoping in the face of disappointment and delay. The great evangelical writer A.W. Tozer said, "The Christian who is seeking better things and who has to his consternation found himself in a state of complete self-despair need not be discouraged…in this painful chastening we shall not be deserted by our God."

That's why we should never stop hoping: because God loves us He will never desert us. Here are three things "hope" enables you to do:

1. To look to the future with expectation (Hebrews 7:19; Hebrews 6:18-19).

2. To wait patiently for the fulfillment of God's promises (Romans 4:17-21; 8:24-25; Psalm 27:13-14).

3. To praise God while we wait (Psalm 41:11; 41:14)

God loves you. Keep hoping.

Day Ninety

The Road That Leads Home To God

1. The road that leads home to God is built with love. *"For God so loved the world that He gave His only begotten son, that whosoever believes in Him should not perish but have everlasting life"* (John 3:16 NKJV).

2. The road that leads home to God is paved with forgiveness. *"If we confess our sins He is faithful and just to forgive us our sins and to cleanse us from all unrighteousness"* (1 John 1:9 NKJV).

3. The road that leads home to God starts at the cross. *"I am the good shepherd. The good shepherd gives his life for the sheep"* (John 10:11). *"...And they took Jesus and led Him away...into a place called Golgotha where they crucified Him"* (John 19:16-18 NKJV). *"But God demonstrates His love for us in that while we were yet sinners Christ died for us"* (Romans 5:8 NKJV).

4. You get on the road that leads home to God by faith and repentance. *"The wages of sin is death; but the gift of God is eternal life through Jesus Christ our Lord"* (Romans 6:23 KJV). *"...what shall we do? Repent and let every one of you be baptized in the name of Jesus Christ..."* (Acts 2:37-38 NKJV). *"...sirs, what must I do to be saved? Believe on the Lord Jesus Christ and you will be saved, and your house"* (Acts 16:30-31 NKJV). *"That if you confess with your mouth the Lord Jesus, and believe in your heart that God raised Him from the dead, you will be saved"* (Romans 10:9 NKJV).

5. The road that leads home to God is a narrow road. *"Enter through the narrow gate. For wide is the gate and broad is the road that leads to destruction, and many enter through it. But small is the gate and narrow the road that leads to life, and only a few find it"* (Matthew 7:13-14 *NIV). "Jesus said…I am the way, the truth, and the life; No one comes to the Father except through me"* (John 14:6 NKJV).

Are you on the right road?

Why am I here? What is my purpose?

If you're like most people, you have a lot of questions you would like to have answered: Questions like, "Who am I?" "Why am I here?" "What does the future hold?" "What's life all about anyway?"

I used to ask the same questions. I often found myself sighing, "There's got to be more to life than this." There was an empty, unfulfilled feeling inside of me, a lonely ache in my heart. I tried just about everything to fill up that emptiness but nothing worked.

I was depressed, lonely, confused…and the merry-go-round I was riding on wouldn't stop to let me off! I was ready to give up on life. After trying everything I could think of there was still something missing. My life had no meaning. The emptiness was still there.

After trying everything else I turned to God for help. I was born again when I received Jesus as my Lord and Savior. He answered my questions. He filled the emptiness in my heart. He gave me peace, love and purpose in life. And I know He wants to do the same thing for you!

The Bible says that *"God loved the world so much that He gave His only begotten Son so that anyone who believes in Him shall not perish but have eternal life"* (John 3:16). Jesus said of Himself, *"I am the Way - yes, and the Truth and the Life, No one can come to the Father except by Me"* (John 14:6). He said, *"I have come that you might have life and have it abundantly"* (John 10:10).

I'm glad you decided to read this brief message. Now, my prayer is that you will do what I did - enter into a personal relationship with God by receiving Jesus Christ as your Savior.

There would never be a better time than right now to accept God's offer of love and forgiveness... *"For the wages of sin is death, but the gift of God is eternal life through Jesus Christ our Lord"* (Romans 6:23).

Have you decided to accept God's offer? Here's how to do it:

Believe on the Lord Jesus (Romans 10:9)

Repent or turn from the old way of life (Luke 13:3)

Confess your sins and ask God to forgive you (1 John 1:9)

Ask Jesus to save you (Romans 10:13)

If you are really sincere, say a prayer like this one:

God, I know I'm a sinner and I need forgiveness. I ask you to forgive my sins. Jesus, I open the door of my life to you and receive you as my Savior.

Are your sins really forgiven? Did Jesus really come into your life? Here's what the Bible says: *"If we confess our sins He forgives us and cleanses us from all unrighteousness"* (1 John 1:9). *"Behold I stand at the door and knock. If anyone opens the door I will come in"* (Revelation 3:20).

This is just the beginning of a new life for you! Try to find a good church, where you can share your experience with other Christians.